DINOSAURS

DINOSAURS

LEARN ABOUT EARTH'S PREHISTORIC CREATURES

Silver Dolphin

San Diego, California

Silver Dolphin Books
An imprint of the Advantage Publishers Group
5880 Oberlin Drive, San Diego, CA 92121-4794
www.silverdolphinbooks.com

Editorial and design by
Amber Books Ltd
74–77 White Lion Street
London N1 9PF
United Kingdom
www.amberbooks.co.uk

ISBN-13: 978-1-59223-600-8
ISBN-10: 1-59223-600-6

Made in China

1 2 3 4 5 10 09 08 07 06

Authors: Per Christiansen and Chris McNab
Design: Jerry Williams

Picture Credits
Illustrations © De Agostini UK Ltd and IMP AB
Except: 40–41, 74–75, 146–147, 174–175 (Photos.com);
106–107 (Altrendo Nature/Getty Images)

Contents

Sticker Fun

Welcome to this exciting and uniquely interactive book. On the pages that follow are fascinating facts about the incredible world of the dinosaurs, from giant vegetarians bigger than a house to ferocious killers with jaws that could snap up a human in a single bite.

Beginning with the wide range of dinosaurs that ruled the earth during the Mesozoic era, this book also includes some of the amazing creatures that lived at this time, such as giant flying reptiles and monster crocodiles. Throughout the book are yellow "Up Close" pages, which feature close looks at some of the more interesting animals.

But this is no ordinary book! To make it even more fun, only the outlines of some creatures are shown, so you get to complete the page by adding the sticker of that animal.

The Carnotaurus sticker from the back of the book fits into the outline on page 64 . . .

Desert plain

Wide-open plains like this were usually home to large groups of dinosaurs struggling to survive in the harsh conditions. Centrosauruses would roam in herds looking for food while a Psittacosaurus would dig up roots with its beak. Create your own desert scene with your dinosaur stickers.

Carcharodontosaurus

Giganotosaurus

Carnotaurus

Deinocheirus

Baryonyx

Metriacanthosaurus

Struthiosaurus

Panoplosaurus

Scelidosaurus

Kentrosaurus

. . . or you could use it in your own imaginative prehistoric scene!

At the back of the book you will find 16 pages of stickers. Each dinosaur or prehistoric beast you'll need is labeled, and they all appear in the order they are featured in the book, so you should find it easy to match them up!

Once you've read the book and placed all the stickers in the right places, you can have even more fun with them because they can be used again and again. We've included five scenes like the one shown above. These show typical prehistoric landscapes where dinosaurs might have lived. Use the stickers to create your own prehistoric panorama on each of these scenes. Using what you've learned in this book, you can match the creatures with the environments they once inhabited— or you can create your own imaginative scenes with any stickers you choose!

All About Dinosaurs

For over 150 million years, dinosaurs ruled the world. They were the greatest, most terrifying, and strongest beasts ever to walk the earth. Yet they came in an amazing variety of shapes, sizes, and behaviors. The dinosaur Euparkeria, for example, was only 20 inches long, ran quickly on two hind legs, and ate other small animals. Jump to the other end of the

Dimetrodon

scale, and you find a creature such as Sauroposeidon. This long-necked monster stretched 102 feet long, weighed a colossal 59 tons, walked on four legs the size of tree trunks, and ate leaves and other vegetation. No wonder it is named after Poseidon, the Greek god of the seas and earthquakes.

What were the dinosaurs?
The name "dinosaur" was coined in 1842 by the British paleontologist Sir Richard Owen—it means "terrible lizard." Dinosaurs lived during the Mesozoic era, which was about 248 to 65 million years ago.

All dinosaurs were reptiles, which meant that they had skeletons and backbones, breathed air, and usually lived on land. As far as we know, most dinosaurs laid eggs rather than giving birth to live young. These eggs could be enormous! The eggs of a dinosaur called Hypselosaurus were each a foot long, weighed over 15 pounds, and held half a gallon of fluid.

Scientists believe that most dinosaurs were cold-

Brachiosaurus

Dimetrodon, for example, had a huge "sail" of skin arching up from its back. It used this sail to catch the sun's rays and warm up its body in the morning, but Dimetrodon could also release body heat through its sail if it was too hot. Dinosaurs were different from other reptiles at the time because they had legs that were positioned underneath the body, whereas many reptiles had legs sticking out from the sides of the body. Some dinosaurs walked on two legs, some on four legs, and some could walk using either two or four legs. Dinosaurs were also digitigrade creatures—this means that they walked on their toes in the same way birds do today.

blooded animals, which means that their body temperature changed according to the temperature of the environment. Some dinosaurs had special body features that helped them stay at the right temperature.

DINOSAUR BEHAVIOR
Dinosaurs were generally either carnivores (meat-eaters) or herbivores (plant-eaters). What they ate

Coelophysis

affected both their body shape and behavior. Meat-eaters had to be fast in order to catch their prey and also had to be able to kill their victims. Utahraptor, for instance, ran quickly on its powerful hind limbs, bringing down its victims with 15-inch-long slashing claws and sharp, serrated teeth. Larger carnivores, such as the famous Tyrannosaurus rex, could not move as fast, so they probably relied more on ambushing their victims. Large carnivores may have lived alone or in small groups, but small carnivores probably hunted in packs to bring down large prey.

Plant-eaters were usually (but not always) slower than carnivores. For example, Apatosaurus was 90 feet long and weighed 30 tons. It walked on four enormous legs, scraping leaves off the highest branches of trees. Because herbivores were vulnerable to predators, they tended to live in large herds in order to reduce each individual's chances of being eaten. Many herbivores may have also migrated during winter months in search of better food and warmer climates.

THE END OF THE DINOSAURS

There were many different types of dinosaurs and prehistoric creatures, and they were found on land, in the seas, and in the air. Sea creatures were dominant during the Triassic period (248–210 million years ago), whereas land dinosaurs were most common during the Jurassic (210–140 million years ago) and Cretaceous (140–65 million years ago) periods.

However, at the end of the Cretaceous period, the dinosaurs became extinct. We still don't know what happened. Some scientists believe that a massive meteorite strike or volcano eruption changed the earth's climate so much that dinosaurs could no longer survive. Others say that important plant species died out, causing the herbivores to starve, which in turn killed the carnivores that fed on them. Whatever the case, the dinosaurs disappeared and the planet entered a new

Giganotosaurus

era. Today we only know about dinosaurs through fossils—parts of animals that have been preserved in the earth over thousands of years. New fossils are being discovered all the time, bringing to life amazing beasts previously lost in time.

Triassic and Jurassic Prosauropods

The prosauropods were a very important group of dinosaurs that thrived at the beginning of the Age of Dinosaurs. They were the first dinosaurs to grow to enormous sizes and they were also the first to specialize in eating plants—all the earlier dinosaurs had been meat-eaters. There were many different kinds of prosauropods—some were small while others weighed as much as a fully grown elephant.

The earliest prosauropods lived 230 million years ago, in the middle of the Triassic period. They were small animals that weighed no more than 20 to 30 pounds, and most walked on their long hind legs. Later forms became so large that they walked on all fours. All prosauropods had sturdy bodies and long, thin necks with small heads. Scientists think their teeth were used to bite off leaves, but they could not chew—they ate mostly ferns and leaves. Inside their stomachs they had a muscular gizzard, like those of modern birds, which contained stones they had swallowed. With their gizzard they could grind the food to an easily digestible pulp.

For reasons unknown, the prosauropods died out early in the Jurassic period, just as dinosaurs were becoming common across much of the earth.

Coloradisaurus

kol-oh-RAHD-uh-SAWR-us

Coloradisaurus walked on four legs but stood on its rear legs to feed on leaves from high branches. It also defended itself on two legs, swiping at attackers with its clawed upper limbs.

FACT-TASTIC

The name Euskelosaurus means "good leg lizard." It was one of the largest animals ever to walk the earth at the time.

Euskelosaurus

yoo-skel-o-SAWR-us

Euskelosaurus ate huge amounts of foliage and could strip a whole area of its vegetation. It used its heavy tail for balance when standing on its rear legs.

Melanorosaurus

muh-LAN-or-o-SAWR-us

Melanorosaurus could grow to a length of 39 feet. It had spoon-shaped teeth that were ideal for raking leaves off branches.

Did you know?
Mussaurus means "mouse lizard."
This is appropriate, as the babies
were no larger than a rat.

Mussaurus
moo-SAWR-us
A newborn Mussaurus measured only
7 to 15 inches. It is thought that many
Mussauruses were eaten by predators
before they reached adulthood.

Riojasaurus
ree-OH-ha-SAWR-us
A fully grown Riojasaurus could weigh up
to four and a half tons. Because it was so
massive, it was unable to stand on its back
legs to feed as other prosauropods did.

▶UP CLOSE: **Mussaurus**

Mussaurus lived in South America 220 million years ago. The first Mussaurus fossils discovered were those of babies. This discovery helped scientists figure out how dinosaurs reproduced and how they cared for their young.

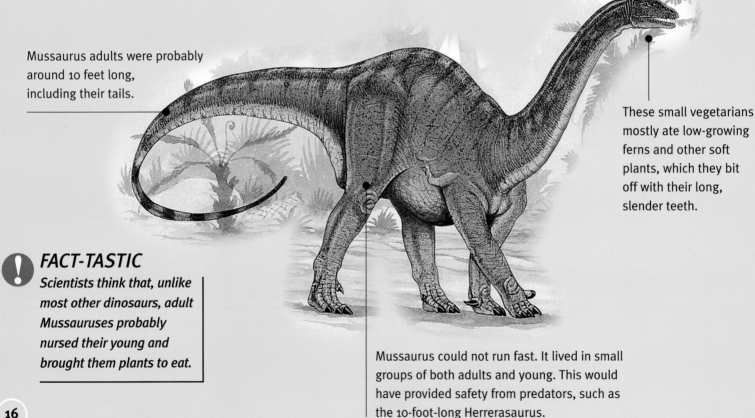

Mussaurus adults were probably around 10 feet long, including their tails.

These small vegetarians mostly ate low-growing ferns and other soft plants, which they bit off with their long, slender teeth.

❗ FACT-TASTIC

Scientists think that, unlike most other dinosaurs, adult Mussauruses probably nursed their young and brought them plants to eat.

Mussaurus could not run fast. It lived in small groups of both adults and young. This would have provided safety from predators, such as the 10-foot-long Herrerasaurus.

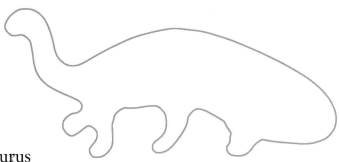

Sellosaurus

SELL-o-SAWR-us

Sellosaurus stored food in large cheek pouches while it was chewing other food. It had a claw on its thumb, used to grab branches and fight off predators.

Thecodontosaurus

THEE-co-dont-oh-SAWR-us

Thecodontosaurus was particularly agile because of its small size—it grew to only around seven feet in length. When threatened, it stood up and sprinted away.

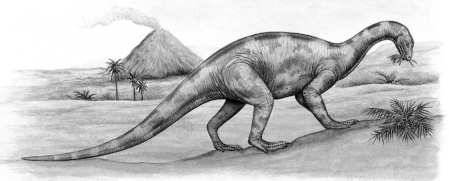

Ammosaurus

am-o-SAWR-us

Ammosaurus lived around 190 million years ago. When attacked, it raised itself onto its back legs and swiped at the predator with sharp front claws and a thumb spike.

Triassic and Jurassic Prosauropods

Anchisaurus

an-key-SAWR-us

Like many plant-eating dinosaurs, Anchisaurus swallowed small stones, or gastroliths. The gastroliths helped grind up the plant food in the dinosaur's stomach.

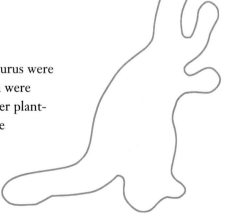

Yunnanosaurus

YOU-nahn-o-SAWR-us

Yunnanosaurus was well equipped to gather plant food. It had a long neck and its feet had five toes, each with a sharp claw.

Lufengosaurus

loo-feng-o-SAWR-us

The fossils of Lufengosaurus were found in China. Its teeth were spikier than those of other plant-eating dinosaurs, so some scientists think it may have also eaten meat.

18

▶UP CLOSE: **Lufengosaurus**

Lufengosaurus lived in China around 200 to 210 million years ago. It is one of the best known of all prosauropods because so many fossils have been found.

Its long, slender jaws were full of small, spoon-shaped teeth, suitable for biting off leaves but not for chewing.

Lufengosaurus mostly walked on all fours. It had a sturdy body and powerful claws on its hands, especially its thumbs.

❗ FACT-TASTIC

Lufengosaurus's claws would have been useful not only for gripping branches but also for fighting off predators.

Lufengosaurus chewed its food with a muscular gizzard in the stomach, which had stones in it, like the stomachs of many birds today.

Jurassic Sauropods

The sauropods were the largest animals ever to walk the earth—the largest ones weighed over 50 tons! They originated in the Triassic period, but scientists do not know much about the early history of sauropods. They became more common in the early part of the Jurassic, and soon they were found all over the world.

All sauropods were large, sturdy animals with legs like columns—just like elephants today. They had long, slender necks, small heads, and very long tails, and they all ate plants. However, we know that they were not all alike. Some could lift their necks high into the air and probably grazed on the tops of trees like giraffes, while others fed close to the ground.

Scientists have found thousands of sauropod footprints all over the world, and these show that many of these dinosaurs lived and moved in herds. This would offer good protection from large, meat-eating dinosaurs.

In the late Jurassic, the sauropods were some of the most common dinosaurs. Many different kinds of sauropods lived alongside each other, and this is evidence that they ate different kinds of plants—otherwise they could not have been so common. Toward the end of the Jurassic, many of the sauropods began to die out.

Jurassic Sauropods

Apatosaurus

ah-PAT-o-SAWR-us

Apatosaurus was for a long time mistakenly called Brontosaurus. It was a mighty dinosaur, growing up to 90 feet in length and weighing a hefty 30 tons.

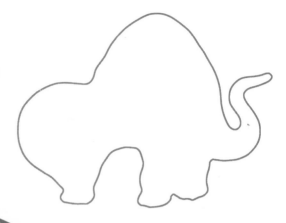

Did you know?
Although giant sauropods used their long tails for support, they couldn't have used them for lashing out at predators without injuring their backs.

Barapasaurus

buh-RAH-pah-SAWR-us

Evidence from fossils found in India shows that Barapasaurus lived together in herds. This lowered each animal's chances of being eaten by predators.

Bothriospondylus

BOTH-ree-o-SPON-di-lus

Bothriospondylus had its nostrils positioned on the top of its nose. This meant that it could eat vegetation without breathing in pieces of leaves.

Cetiosaurus

SEAT-ee-oh-SAWR-us

Cetiosaurus probably lived near water. This isn't how it got its name (which means "whale lizard"), however—that was due to the shape of its backbone.

Brachiosaurus

brack-ee-uh-SAWR-us

As an adult, the giant Brachiosaurus had no enemies. It would have been too dangerous for another predator to attack such a huge animal.

Cetiosauriscus

SEE-tie-o-saw-RIS-kus

When Cetiosauriscus was feeding, it often stood on its hind legs, using its long tail for support.

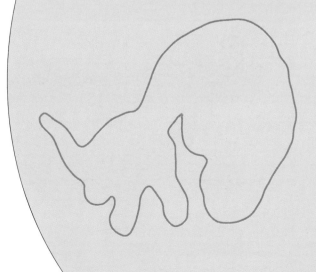

▶UP CLOSE: **Brachiosaurus**

Brachiosaurus was a gigantic sauropod that looked a bit like an enormous giraffe. It weighed up to 50 tons and stood more than 40 feet tall!

Brachiosaurus ate in a peculiar manner. Sometimes it bit the leaves off the branches, but other times it raked them off by pulling its head backward.

Brachiosaurus's mouth was designed for eating massive amounts of vegetation. It had a total of 52 chisel-shaped teeth in its mouth.

Brachiosaurus was so tall that it could always find food high in the trees, even during droughts. Other sauropods could not reach so high into the treetops.

! *FACT-TASTIC*

Brachiosaurus lived on the open plains of North America and Africa around 150 million years ago, feeding off the treetops.

Datousaurus

dah-toe-SAWR-us

Datousaurus used to travel around in herds. Any predators that attacked the herd faced being crushed by the tails and bodies of these 50-foot-long creatures.

Diplodocus

di-PLOD-o-kus

Diplodocus had a total of 15 vertebrae in its neck. These were hollow bones—if they had been solid, the dinosaur would have been unable to lift its own neck.

Dicraeosaurus

die-CREE-oh-SAWR-us

Dicraeosaurus's teeth were not made for chewing. Instead they stripped off leaves and branches whole, which were then broken down by acids in the dinosaur's stomach.

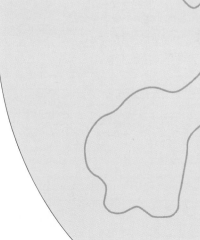

25

▶UP CLOSE: **Diplodocus**

Diplodocus was a huge sauropod and could reach a length of 92 feet. But it was slender in build and probably weighed only 15 to 18 tons.

Most of the time Diplodocus fed close to the ground, since its neck was not very flexible.

Diplodocus could use its tail as a prop when the animal reared up on its hind limbs to reach for the juiciest leaves.

❗ FACT-TASTIC
Diplodocus's teeth were long and thin and were only present at the front of the mouth. It tore at leaves rather than biting them.

By standing on its hind limbs, it could reach up to 30 feet into the treetops!

Euhelopus

you-HEL-oh-pus

The name Euhelopus means "good marsh foot." The dinosaur was so called because its wide, flat feet kept it from sinking into the soft ground of marshlands and floodplains.

Haplocanthosaurus

hap-lo-KAN-tho-SAWR-us

Many sauropods had hollow bones in the neck to make the neck lighter. Haplocanthosaurus, however, had bones that were almost solid, so it struggled to lift its head above its shoulders.

Kotasaurus

KOHT-ah-SAWR-us

Long-necked dinosaurs like Kotasaurus needed a long tail for balance as they walked. The 30-foot-long Kotasaurus would have spent most of its day feeding just to stay alive.

Jurassic Sauropods

Seismosaurus, discovered in New Mexico in 1991, is believed to be the largest dinosaur ever to have lived.

Lapparentosaurus

la-pah-RENT-o-SAWR-us

Only the fossilized skeleton of a young Lapparentosaurus has been found. Scientists think it would have taken 12 years for Lapparentosaurus to grow to its full, enormous adult size.

Omeisaurus

OH-may-SAWR-us

Pictures of Omeisaurus often show a club at the end of the tail. Paleontologists now think this image is wrong, and that a skeleton of the Omeisaurus was mixed up with the tail of a nearby Shunosaurus.

Did you know?

Lapparentosaurus was discovered on the island of Madagascar, which is home to more than 5 percent of the world's different species.

Seismosaurus

SIZE-moe-SAWR-us

Seismosaurus means "earthquake lizard." It's an apt name—the creature was up to 148 feet long and weighed up to 33 tons.

Shunosaurus

SHOO-no-SAWR-us

Shunosaurus had a solid club at the end of its long, strong tail. Any predator whacked by this heavy weapon was likely to be badly injured or even killed.

Ultrasaurus

UL-trah-SAWR-us

Only a few fossilized bones of Ultrasaurus have been discovered. The size of these bones, however, have led paleontologists to estimate that the dinosaur grew to 98 feet long and 30 tons in weight.

Cretaceous Sauropods

In the Jurassic period, the sauropods were the dominant plant-eaters throughout much of the world. But toward the end of the Jurassic, many died out. In the Cretaceous period, new kinds of plant-eating dinosaurs appeared and began competing with the remaining sauropods.

Sauropods had been common all over the world in the Jurassic, but in the Cretaceous they mostly lived in the south, on the supercontinent scientists call Gondwana. This landmass was made up of present-day South America, Africa, Australia, and parts of Asia. The Cretaceous sauropods were also different from the Jurassic ones. Most of them belonged to a new group called the titanosaurs. They had sturdier bodies and legs than many of the Jurassic sauropods, but their necks and tails were shorter.

Many of the titanosaurs also evolved armor. In their skin were embedded round, bony plates, called scutes, which offered good protection from the many kinds of large, meat-eating dinosaurs that lived in the Cretaceous. Like most sauropods, the Cretaceous titanosaurs also found safety in size. Most were so large that any meat-eater would think twice before attacking them. The young were vulnerable, however, and many were probably killed by predators before they were fully grown.

Cretaceous Sauropods

Aeolosaurus
EE-oh-lo-SAWR-us
Aeolosaurus was a herd dinosaur, living in groups for protection and feeding. The herds would migrate to new feeding areas depending on the season.

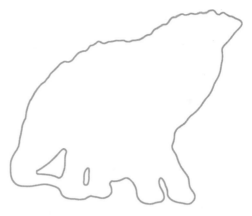

Amargasaurus
uh-MARG-uh-SAWR-us
Amargasaurus had two rows of spines running down the length of its back. Growing up to 20 inches long, these spines would have provided some defense against being bitten by a predator.

Alamosaurus
al-uh-moe-SAWR-us
Fossils of Alamosaurus have been found in New Mexico in the southwestern United States. Alamosaurus could grow up to 28 feet long from nose to tail.

▶UP CLOSE: **Amargasaurus**

Amargasaurus lived in South America around 130 million years ago and was a relative of Diplodocus. Scientists think that it probably fed on soft, low-growing ferns.

! *FACT-TASTIC*

Amargasaurus's spikes run in pairs down the dinosaur's back, so it might have had two sails—or none!

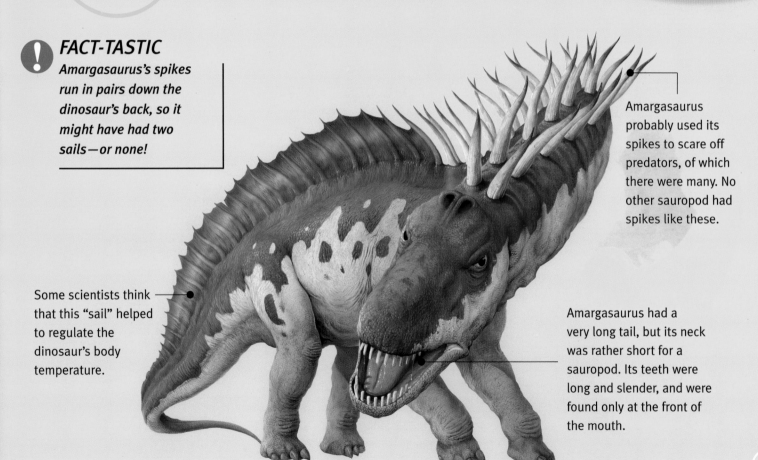

Amargasaurus probably used its spikes to scare off predators, of which there were many. No other sauropod had spikes like these.

Some scientists think that this "sail" helped to regulate the dinosaur's body temperature.

Amargasaurus had a very long tail, but its neck was rather short for a sauropod. Its teeth were long and slender, and were found only at the front of the mouth.

33

Cretaceous Sauropods

Argentinosaurus

ahr-gen-TEEN-oh-SAWR-us

Argentinosaurus is the largest dinosaur of any type that has ever been discovered. Only a portion of a fossil has been found to date.

Antarctosaurus

ant-ARK-toe-SAWR-us

Antarctosaurus could stretch up and pull leaves off branches that were 20 feet above the ground. It had teeth only at the front of its mouth, so it was unable to chew its food.

Hypselosaurus

HIP-sel-oh-SAWR-us

Hypselosaurus eggs were 12 inches long and could hold half a gallon of fluid. The dinosaur laid these eggs in a straight line either during walking or by nudging them into place with its foot.

▶UP CLOSE: **Argentinosaurus**

Argentinosaurus was a true colossus—the largest land animal that ever lived. Even though Argentinosaurus lived alongside gigantic predatory dinosaurs, it would have had no enemies as an adult. It was so large that it would simply have been too dangerous to attack it.

FACT-TASTIC

One of the Argentinosaurus vertebrae (bones of the spine and neck) found measured an amazing 5 feet 6 inches across.

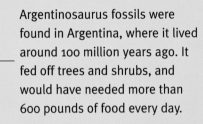

Argentinosaurus fossils were found in Argentina, where it lived around 100 million years ago. It fed off trees and shrubs, and would have needed more than 600 pounds of food every day.

Argentinosaurus was 115 feet long and weighed 75 tons! Its thighbone was more than eight feet long.

Argentinosaurus laid eggs on the ground. The young were so small compared to the adults that scientists think the adults did not look after them.

Cretaceous Sauropods

Magyarosaurus
MAG-yar-o-SAWR-us

Magyarosaurus was a small sauropod—it grew up to "only" 26 feet long. It may have been smaller than other types of sauropods because it lived in a region with fewer predators.

! FACT-TASTIC

Magyarosaurus is named after the Hungarian word for "Hungary," and is a reference to the place where it was found.

Nemegtosaurus
NAY-meg-toe-SAWR-us

Little is known about Nemegtosaurus, whose fossilized bones were found in Mongolia. It had a very wide body, but its slender neck could push into thick foliage for feeding.

Neuquensaurus
NOO-kwen-SAWR-us

Neuquensaurus had a skin that was covered with bony plates. These plates protected the dinosaur and also deterred predators from attacking in the first place.

Opisthocoelicaudia

oh-PIS-tho-SEEL-ih-CAWD-ee-ah

Opisthocoelicaudia was a stocky, forest-dwelling dinosaur. Large herds of these animals would gather together for protection, and each would eat up to 140 pounds of food each day.

Pelorosaurus

pe-LOW-roh-SAWR-us

Pelorosaurus had bony, six-sided plates on its skin for added protection.

Quaesitosaurus

kway-ZEET-oh-SAWR-us

Having a long neck was very useful for Quaesitosaurus. It could stand on firm ground and stretch its neck out to reach vegetation located over soft, marshy ground.

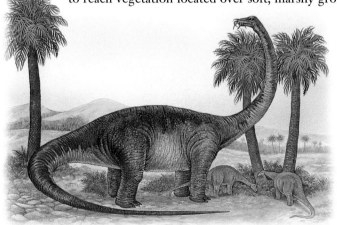

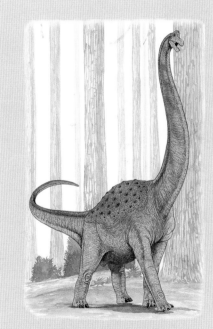

Cretaceous Sauropods

Did you know?
In 1997, several thousand fossil dinosaur eggs were found in Patagonia, Argentina. They are believed to have been laid by a herd of Saltasauruses.

Saltasaurus
SALT-ah-SAWR-us
Saltasaurus was a 40-foot-long armored plant-eater. It lived about 79 to 83 million years ago.

Titanosaurus
tie-TAN-oh-SAWR-us
Weighing up to 14 tons and standing 10 feet tall at the hips, Titanosaurus would have eaten literally tons of vegetation every week.

▶UP CLOSE: **Saltasaurus**

Compared to other titanosaurs, Saltasaurus was rather small. It lived in South America around 80 million years ago and weighed three to four tons.

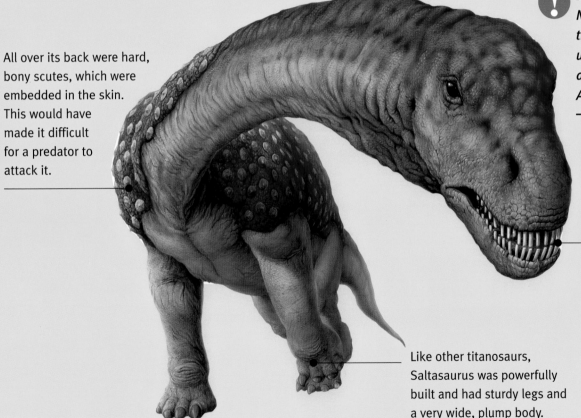

All over its back were hard, bony scutes, which were embedded in the skin. This would have made it difficult for a predator to attack it.

! FACT-TASTIC
No complete skull of a titanosaur had been found until 1996, when one was discovered in Patagonia, Argentina.

No complete skull of a Saltasaurus has been found, but it probably had long, peglike teeth to strip leaves off branches.

Like other titanosaurs, Saltasaurus was powerfully built and had sturdy legs and a very wide, plump body.

Grassy plain

Large herds of giant herbivores such as Diplodocus once roamed the lush, open forests and plains, stalked by predators such as the terrifying Tyrannosaurus rex. Create your own grassy country scene with your dinosaur stickers.

Early Predatory Dinosaurs

The predatory dinosaurs are also known as theropods. This means "beast-footed," but their feet actually looked similar to a bird's feet. Like birds, all theropods used their toes only for support while the rest of the foot was raised off the ground. This made them long-legged and capable of running fast, like ostriches today. Their arms were not used for running but for grasping prey. All theropods had long skulls and jaws full of pointed teeth with jagged edges, like a steak knife.

Some of the earliest known dinosaurs are predators. The most primitive and earliest species lived nearly 235 million years ago and were no larger than a turkey. These early theropods had four fingers on their grasping hands, but all later species had just three fingers. The early theropods were slower and longer-limbed than later species, and were also smaller.

Throughout their evolution, most theropods remained small, but some grew to immense sizes and weighed as much as an elephant. Such creatures must have been truly frightening, and it is no wonder that many plant-eating dinosaurs evolved a whole arsenal of horns, bony clubs, and armor to protect themselves.

Early Predatory Dinosaurs

Coelophysis
SEE-low-FIE-sis

In one area of the southwestern United States, 100 fossilized Coelophysis skeletons were found. This group of agile, fast-moving predators probably drowned in a flash flood.

Ceratosaurus
ser-RAT-uh-SAWR-us

Ceratosaurus had a large "horn-blade" on its nose. The blade grew bigger as the dinosaur grew older, but Ceratosaurus's real weapons were its teeth and four-fingered claws.

Dilophosaurus
die-LOF-oh-SAWR-us

Dilophosaurus had hollow bones to give it a lightweight skeleton. With its pistonlike legs Dilophosaurus could run down its prey, which it seized with its claws.

▶UP CLOSE: **Dilophosaurus**

Dilophosaurus was one of the largest of the early predatory dinosaurs. It lived in North America 200 million years ago and was 20 to 26 feet long.

Dilophosaurus probably hunted the prosauropods that were common at the time. It used its large, clawed hands to grasp its prey, and killed it with its long, sharp teeth.

On top of the head were two long, thin crests, which may have been used for display.

It was slender in build, and would have weighed only 600 to 700 pounds.

! ***FACT-TASTIC***
In the film Jurassic Park, *Dilophosaurus had a neck frill and was able to spit venom out of its mouth, but this is pure fiction.*

Herrerasaurus

huh-RARE-ah-SAWR-us

Herrerasaurus used to hide among the vegetation until the moment was right to rush out and ambush passing prey.

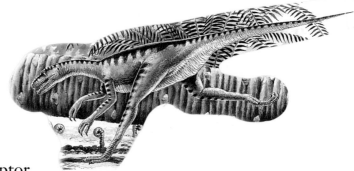

Eoraptor

EE-oh-RAP-tor

Eoraptor lived around 228 million years ago. Fossilized bones of this dinosaur have mainly been found in South America.

Liliensternus

LIL-ee-in-STER-nus

Liliensternus had vicious claws on its hands and feet. It would hunt as part of a pack, which was capable of killing a large, herbivorous dinosaur.

▶UP CLOSE: Eoraptor

Eoraptor is the oldest predatory dinosaur to be discovered. It was only three feet long and weighed around 10 pounds. All the later and more advanced predatory dinosaurs evolved from creatures such as Eoraptor.

Like other predators, Eoraptor had knifelike teeth in its jaws. However, at the front of the mouth its teeth were more spoon-shaped, almost like those of prosauropods.

Eoraptors belonged to a larger group of dinosaurs called saurischians, or lizard-hipped dinosaurs. Their hip bones were similar to those of modern lizards.

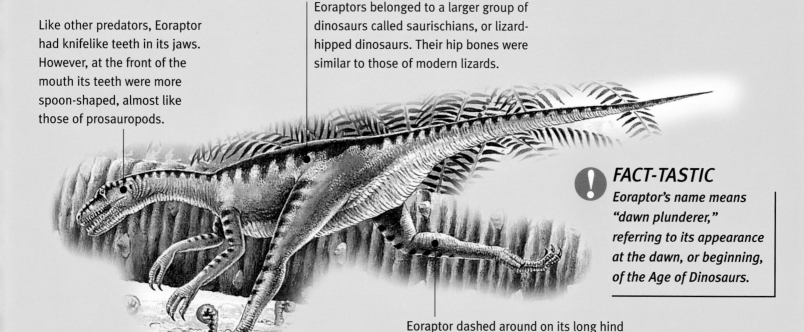

! FACT-TASTIC
Eoraptor's name means "dawn plunderer," referring to its appearance at the dawn, or beginning, of the Age of Dinosaurs.

Eoraptor dashed around on its long hind legs and used its grasping hands to catch small lizards and large insects.

Early Predatory Dinosaurs

Proceratosaurus
pro-ser-RAT-uh-SAWR-us
Proceratosaurus had a crest on the front of its nose and teeth that were designed to grab and hold slippery fish—it hunted along rivers.

Did you know?
Saltopus is probably the smallest dinosaur yet discovered. It might have been as small as 10 inches tall when fully grown.

Saltopus
SALT-oh-pus
Saltopus was very fast, with quick reflexes to sprint after lizards and large insects and to escape from predators.

 FACT-TASTIC
Staurikosaurus is named after the constellation of the Southern Cross because it was discovered in Brazil, in South America.

Staurikosaurus

STORE-ee-koh-SAWR-us

In its time, Staurikosaurus was probably the fastest land animal on the planet. It would run down its prey and kill it with razor-sharp teeth and claws.

Syntarsus

sin-TAR-sus

Syntarsus lived and hunted in large packs. Each animal grew up to 10 feet in height, and it may have had a plume of feathers covering its head.

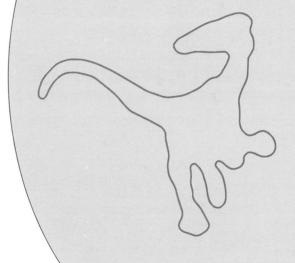

Jurassic Predatory Dinosaurs

In the Jurassic period, theropods became much more common all over the world, and species of many different sizes evolved. Some were no larger than a chicken, while the enormous carnosaurs could weigh several tons.

Jurassic theropods were quite different from the earlier species of the Triassic period. They had longer legs and larger muscles, and their jaws had become stronger, so they could bite harder. Theropods also became larger, which meant they could hunt the great variety of plant-eating dinosaurs that were becoming widespread throughout the world. Some of these plant-eaters, such as the sauropods, were enormous. This meant that the carnivores had to become very large as well—several of them weighed up to five tons, with heads more than three feet long! Some of the Jurassic theropods appear to have lived and hunted in packs, but scientists say that most were likely to have been solitary hunters.

In the Jurassic, several of the smaller theropods began to evolve into birdlike creatures. Scientists think that many of them probably had feathers all over their bodies and were warm-blooded, like birds and mammals today. Toward the end of the Jurassic, some of those small theropods evolved wings and began to fly. These were the first birds.

Jurassic Predatory Dinosaurs

Allosaurus
al-oh-SAWR-us

Allosaurus was an immensely dangerous predator. It would ambush large, plant-eating animals, using its serrated teeth to take large bites of meat.

FACT-TASTIC

Coelurus fossils were first discovered in Wyoming in 1879. Coelurus was just six feet long and its name means "hollow tail."

Coelurus
see-LURE-us

Coelurus had a very long tail, like a whip. The tail helped the dinosaur to turn quickly when it was running fast, and this ability helped it to catch prey and evade predators.

▶UP CLOSE: **Allosaurus**

Allosaurus is one of the most famous of all the carnivorous dinosaurs. It was a huge predator, up to 30 feet from nose to tail, and weighed more than two tons.

Without its massive tail, which it used as a counterbalance, Allosaurus would have fallen flat on its face!

In Colorado, scientists have found a place where an adult Allosaurus feasted on a sauropod. Also on the bones were tooth marks from babies, which suggests that Allosaurus fed meat to its young.

 **FACT-TASTIC**
Allosaurus probably hunted in packs like wild dogs and wolves today, preying on young and weak sauropods.

Allosaurus had strong arms with large, curved claws on its powerful, three-fingered hands.

53

Jurassic Predatory Dinosaurs

Compsognathus
KOMP-sog-NAY-thus
With its two huge eyes, Compsognathus would have had excellent vision for hunting, even at night.

Cryolophosaurus
krie-o-LOF-o-SAWR-us
The crest on Cryolophosaurus's head was too weak to be a weapon. It was probably used mainly for display, to attract mates.

Gasosaurus
GAS-oh-SAWR-us
Gasosaurus had two main weapons. It had a large mouth with teeth pointed like knives, and it also had very sharp claws on the ends of its three-fingered hands.

▶UP CLOSE: Compsognathus

Compsognathus lived in Europe around 150 million years ago and has been found in the same deposits as the early bird Archaeopteryx. However, Compsognathus probably lived on the ground, whereas Archaeopteryx mainly lived in trees.

A close relative of Compsognathus, called Sinosauropteryx ("Chinese lizard wing"), was found with feathers all over its body. Scientists think that Compsognathus was also feathered.

! FACT-TASTIC
Compsognathus was a tiny, lightweight theropod. Adults reached only three feet in length and weighed just seven pounds.

Lining the birdlike beak of Compsognathus were sharp, serrated teeth, like the edge of a saw.

Compsognathus used its long claws to feed on small reptiles and mammals and large insects. One Compsognathus fossil was found with a tiny reptile in its stomach.

Megalosaurus

MEG-ah-lo-SAWR-us

Megalosaurus had jaws strong enough to crunch right through to the bone. Its teeth had serrated edges, like steak knives, and these were ideal for slicing through the toughest flesh.

! FACT-TASTIC

Megalosaurus was the first dinosaur to be named, in 1824. Before this, many people believed its bones were those of a giant man!

Ornitholestes

or-NITH-oh-LES-teez

The first Ornitholestes fossil that was found contained a crushed skull. The unfortunate animal may have been trampled by a huge sauropod, rather than having been eaten by a predator.

Did you know?

Ornitholestes was closely related to the ancestors of birds. The design of its wrists meant it could tuck in its arms in the same way that a modern bird folds in its wings.

Szechuanosaurus

sesh-WAHN-uh-SAWR-us

Szechuanosaurus probably hunted its prey in a pack, like wolves and lions do today. It had extremely strong jaw muscles and would have clamped fast onto its prey to bring it down for the kill.

Yangchuanosaurus

YANG-choo-WAN-oh-SAWR-us

Yangchuanosaurus was a fearsome predator that reached up to 33 feet in height. It had a small crest on its skull and a long crest running down its backbone.

Cretaceous Predatory Dinosaurs

The meat-eating dinosaurs had their heyday in the Cretaceous period. We know of more theropods from the late Cretaceous than from any other time during the Age of Dinosaurs. But this is probably because there are a lot more dinosaur fossil sites dating from the Cretaceous period.

By the Cretaceous, the theropods had evolved into a vast number of different species that lived in many different ways. Some were very long-limbed and had small heads and toothless beaks, and mainly fed on plants or small animals. Others were short-limbed and heavy in build and probably only ate plants. Some had large claws on their hands and ate fish, while others lived in deserts and probably hunted small mammals and reptiles. Most species lived on the ground, but scientists think that some of the smaller species may have lived in the trees. Many of the small species were very birdlike and had feathers all over their bodies.

The large theropods reached their high point with the fearsome tyrannosaurs. These were the strongest and most frightening of all the large theropods. The tyrannosaurs lived in Asia and North America, but other large meat-eaters thrived in South America and Africa.

Abelisaurus

ah-BEL-i-SAWR-us

A fast-moving predator, Abelisaurus grew to around 25 feet tall. It was a patient and ferocious hunter.

Afrovenator

AF-roh-vee-NAY-tor

Afrovenator's mouth was packed with deadly teeth—each tooth grew up to two inches long. When running after prey, it held its long tail straight out to provide balance.

Acrocanthosaurus

AK-roh-CAN-thuh-SAWR-us

Acrocanthosaurus had a deep "sail" running down the length of its back. This feature probably helped the dinosaur control its body temperature.

▶UP CLOSE: **Acrocanthosaurus**

Acrocanthosaurus was an enormous predatory dinosaur that lived in North America 115 million years ago. It could reach a length of 40 feet and weigh five tons!

The spines along the sail were up to 18 inches long and may have helped to protect Acrocanthosaurus from attacks by other predators.

 FACT-TASTIC
Acrocanthosaurus had a keen sense of smell. It would have been able to track its victims by scent.

Acrocanthosaurus was the top predator at the time it lived. It mainly hunted large iguanodonts, which it held with its very powerful arms, equipped with large, curved claws.

Acrocanthosaurus's colossal head was more than four feet long. Using its 68 bladelike teeth, it would bite its victim's neck, creating a huge, fatal wound.

Cretaceous Predatory Dinosaurs

Albertosaurus
al-BUR-toe-SAWR-us

Albertosaurus was probably a part-time scavenger. It had a strong sense of smell, which it used to find the bodies of dead dinosaurs. Then it ate the rotting flesh!

Alectrosaurus
ah-LECK-troh-SAWR-us

Alectrosaurus was an early ancestor of the famous Tyrannosaurus rex. It was only half the height of T. rex, but it was just as well armed, with large jaws, lots of teeth, and sharp claws.

Did you know?
In the Cretaceous period, the area of southern England where Baryonyx fossils have been found was covered in steamy, swampy forests.

Alioramus
AL-ee-uh-RAY-mus

Alioramus was another ancestor of T. rex. Its nose, however, was covered with bony knobs and its bite was much weaker than that of other tyrannosaurs.

Aublysodon

aw-BLIS-oh-don

Almost the only fossilized remains found of
Aublysodon are its teeth. Unlike other tyrannosaurs,
Aublysodon's teeth were not serrated, so they would
have been used to stab its prey rather than cut it.

Baryonyx

BAYR-ee-ON-iks

Baryonyx is the only known fish-
eating dinosaur. Each hand had a
single 12-inch claw, which it would
use to spear fish in the water.

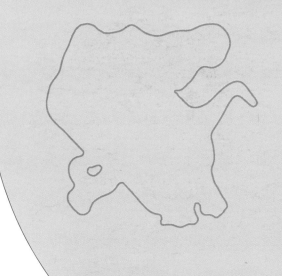

Becklespinax

BECK-el-SPY-nax

Becklespinax had
a heat-regulating
spine along its back,
which helped keep
its body at the right
temperature.

Cretaceous Predatory Dinosaurs

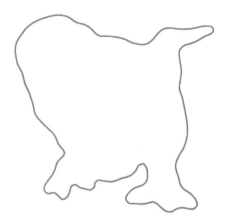

Carnotaurus
KAR-no-TAWR-us
The name Carnotaurus means "flesh-eating bull." The dinosaur was given this name because its large, bumpy eyebrows looked like a bull's horns.

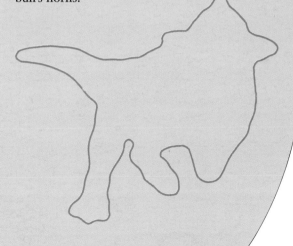

Carcharodontosaurus
kahr-KAR-o-DONT-o-SAWR-us
Fossils of Carcharodontosaurus were first discovered in the 1920s, and more were found in the 1990s. Paleontologists were slow to realize that they had found the largest carnivore that ever lived on land.

Chilantaisaurus
chee-LAWN-ti-SAWR-us
The claws on Chilantaisaurus's hands were shaped like sickles. It used these claws to slash into the body of its prey, cutting muscles and tendons and leaving the victim helpless.

▶UP CLOSE: **Carcharodontosaurus**

Carcharodontosaurus was the largest predatory dinosaur that ever existed. It lived in northern Africa around 100 million years ago and could reach a length of 45 feet—even bigger than the legendary Tyrannosaurus rex.

This fearsome dinosaur's jaws were lined with six- to seven-inch-long knifelike teeth, which had rows of grooves that helped it grip its prey.

Carcharodontosaurus probably held its tail in the air while it ran to provide a balance for the weight of its huge head.

Scientists think that Carcharodontosaurus mainly hunted alone, but its size and strength meant that even large sauropods were in danger when this enormous predator was on the prowl.

! *FACT-TASTIC*
Carcharodontosaurus means "shark-toothed lizard." Its brain was only one-eighth the size of a human's.

Cretaceous Predatory Dinosaurs

Deinocheirus
DINE-oh-KIE-rus

Deinocheirus was a terrifying creature. Its eight-foot-long arms ended in terrifying weapons: 10-inch claws shaped like grappling hooks for slashing at its prey.

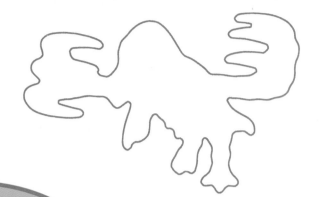

(!) FACT-TASTIC

Dryptosaurus was the first theropod discovered in North America, and was named by paleontologist Othniel C. Marsh in 1877.

Did you know?
All that has been found of Deinocheirus is its immense claws, so scientists can only guess at what the rest of its body looked like.

Dryptosaurus
DRIP-toe-SAWR-us

Dryptosaurus had eight-inch-long claws to back up its huge, crushing jaws. It probably hunted alone, ambushing its victims in areas of dense vegetation.

Erlikosaurus
ER-lik-oh-SAWR-us

Many dinosaurs were closely related to birds. Some scientists think that Erlikosaurus may have actually been covered with feathers.

Eustreptospondylus

you-STREP-toh-SPON-dy-lus

Eustreptospondylus had several holes in its massive skull. Without these holes, the dinosaur's head may have been too heavy for its neck muscles to move easily.

Giganotosaurus

jie-GAN-oh-toe-SAWR-us

Giganotosaurus was even larger than Tyrannosaurus rex. If it were alive today, it could eat a human adult in a single bite!

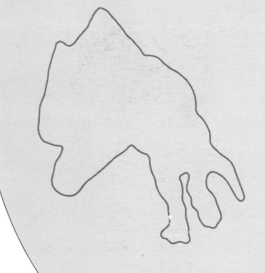

Indosuchus

in-doh-SOOK-us

Indosuchus had a mouth full of serrated teeth that grew up to four inches long. If the dinosaur lost a tooth, a new one would quickly grow in its place.

▶UP CLOSE: **Giganotosaurus**

Giganotosaurus was probably the largest theropod that ever lived. It is a close relative of Allosaurus, and lived in South America around 100 million years ago.

Bony ridges on the head probably protected the eyes, which were essential hunting tools— but they would have reduced the animal's forward vision.

Giganotosaurus had tiny arms that were almost useless. They might have been used to get the dinosaur off the ground or were used during mating.

Its six-inch-long, daggerlike teeth had serrated edges. They were ideal for slicing through flesh!

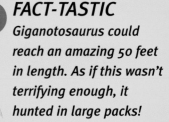

❗ FACT-TASTIC

Giganotosaurus could reach an amazing 50 feet in length. As if this wasn't terrifying enough, it hunted in large packs!

Metriacanthosaurus

MET-ri-ah-CAN-thuh-SAWR-us

Metriacanthosaurus had a ridge of small spines along its backbone, which made it look humpbacked.

Nanshiungosaurus

NAN-shee-ung-ah-SAWR-us

Nanshiungosaurus had teeth like those of a plant-eater, but its claws looked like a predator's. It may have eaten both plants and meat.

Nanotyrannus

NAN-oh-tie-RAN-us

It is possible that fossils of Nanotyrannus might simply be those of a young Tyrannosaurus rex. Like T. rex, it has a large jaw full of serrated teeth and short arms with sharp claws.

Cretaceous Predatory Dinosaurs

Piatnitzkysaurus
pit-NYIT-skee-SAWR-us
Piatnitzkysaurus had sharp teeth, short arms, and powerful legs. It was around 20 feet tall and lived in what is now Argentina.

Spinosaurus
SPINE-oh-SAWR-us
Spinosaurus was a gigantic predator that lived in northern Africa around 100 million years ago. At up to 52 feet in length, it was the longest of all the predatory dinosaurs.

Suchomimus
SOOK-o-MIME-us
Suchomimus was a skilled fish hunter, although its fossils were discovered in 1997 in what is today the Sahara Desert!

▶UP CLOSE: **Spinosaurus**

Spinosaurus may have been large, but compared to other predators at the time it was quite lightweight at just four tons. It probably ate fish, eggs, and other dinosaurs.

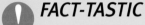

FACT-TASTIC

The lakes in which Spinosaurus fished contained fish up to 12 feet long—more than enough for dinner!

The large sail on Spinosaurus's back helped the dinosaur control its temperature, either by ridding the body of excess heat or by absorbing the sun's warmth.

Spinosaurus was not a predator of large animals. Its skull was very elongated and slender, and its teeth looked like those of crocodiles.

Spinosaurus probably fed mainly on large freshwater fish, which it caught with its long snout and large claws.

71

Cretaceous Predatory Dinosaurs

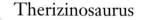

Tarbosaurus
TAR-bow-SAWR-us
Tarbosaurus was an Asian version of Tyrannosaurus rex. Some fossils suggest that Tarbosauruses fought each other for control of territory.

Therizinosaurus
THER-uh-ZEEN-oh-SAWR-us
Therizinosaurus had three huge claws on each hand. The claws were used for grabbing plants and small animals, and also for defense.

Tyrannosaurus rex
tie-RAN-oh-SAWR-us RECKS
Tyrannosaurus rex killed its prey by tearing off chunks of flesh up to three feet long. It could also grab small prey with its hands and shake it to death.

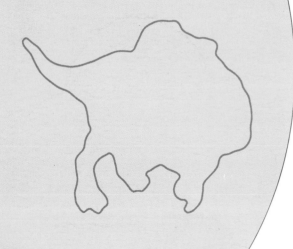

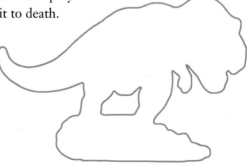

Tyrannosaurus rex was the most powerful of all the predatory dinosaurs. Its head was four and a half feet long and its teeth were the size of bananas!

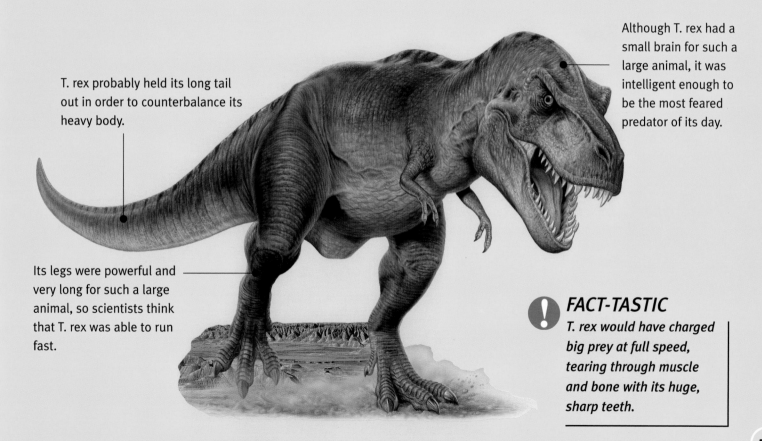

Although T. rex had a small brain for such a large animal, it was intelligent enough to be the most feared predator of its day.

T. rex probably held its long tail out in order to counterbalance its heavy body.

Its legs were powerful and very long for such a large animal, so scientists think that T. rex was able to run fast.

! **FACT-TASTIC**

T. rex would have charged big prey at full speed, tearing through muscle and bone with its huge, sharp teeth.

Rocky hillside

Plant-eating dinosaurs such as Mussaurus once lived on this hilly landscape, and hiding among the boulders would be hungry predators such as Eoraptor. Create your own hillside scene with your dinosaur stickers.

Birdlike Predatory Dinosaurs

During the Jurassic period, many of the smaller species of theropods became more birdlike. And toward the end of the Jurassic, the true birds emerged. They soon became highly specialized for flight, with a lifestyle quite unlike their theropod ancestors, who mainly hunted small animals on the ground.

Many different groups of small theropods took on birdlike features during the Jurassic and Cretaceous periods, but only one group became true birds. The closest dinosaur relatives of birds are known as dromaeosaurs and troodonts. You can see several of them in this book: Deinonychus, Velociraptor, and Troodon are some of the most well known. Although none of them were birds, they had a lot of things in common with our flying friends today. Several of them lived and bred in large colonies. They made round nests on the ground and incubated their eggs. But unlike modern-day birds, many of them had vicious-looking claws on both their hands and feet, and were probably fierce predators.

Birdlike Predatory Dinosaurs

Did you know?
Anserimimus was given its name, which means "goose mimic," when its headless fossil skeleton was discovered in Mongolia.

Adasaurus
ADD-ah-SAWR-us
Adasaurus killed its prey using large, sickle-shaped claws on its feet. When it was walking or running, it would hold the claws off the ground to avoid damaging them.

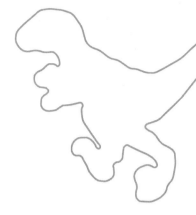

Anserimimus
AN-ser-i-MIME-us
Anserimimus looked a lot like an ostrich, with long legs and a long neck. It grew to only around three feet in length and probably ate dinosaur eggs or small animals.

❗ FACT-TASTIC
Borogovia was named after the Borogove, a fictional bird from the Alice in Wonderland stories by Lewis Carroll.

Alvarezsaurus
al-vuh-rez-SAWR-us
Alvarezsaurus had long, birdlike legs and could run extremely fast when it was hunting prey.

Archaeornithomimus
AHR-kee-or-NITH-oh-MIME-us
Using evidence from footprints found in China, paleontologists determined that Archaeornithomimus could run at speeds of up to 43 miles per hour.

Borogovia
bor-oh-GOH-vee-a
Borogovia had long arms with three-clawed hands. It would ambush its prey, leaping out from behind vegetation and grabbing the victim with its claws.

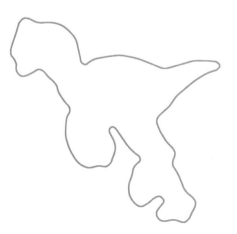

Chirostenotes
KIE-roh-STEN-oh-teez
Chirostenotes had a birdlike head and feet. Some species of the dinosaur had a large crest on the head, while others had no crest at all.

Birdlike Predatory Dinosaurs

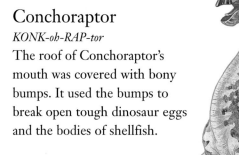

Conchoraptor
KONK-oh-RAP-tor
The roof of Conchoraptor's mouth was covered with bony bumps. It used the bumps to break open tough dinosaur eggs and the bodies of shellfish.

Deinonychus
die-NON-ih-kus
Deinonychus had a five-inch retractable claw on the second toe of each foot. Its tail was long and rigid to provide it with balance.

▶UP CLOSE: **Deinonychus**

Deinonychus was a dromaeosaur and was closely related to birds. Like all dromaeosaurs, it had very long arms and huge claws on its hands.

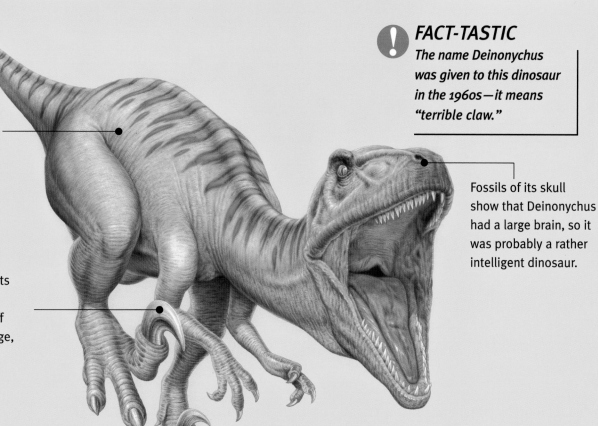

Although Deinonychus was less than 10 feet long and weighed only around 100 pounds, it was a fearsome hunter. It lived and hunted in packs, and could kill animals that were 10 times its own size!

Deinonychus ran on only its third and fourth toes. Toe number two was raised off the ground and bore a huge, sickle-shaped claw.

! FACT-TASTIC

The name Deinonychus was given to this dinosaur in the 1960s—it means "terrible claw."

Fossils of its skull show that Deinonychus had a large brain, so it was probably a rather intelligent dinosaur.

Birdlike Predatory Dinosaurs

Gallimimus

gal-uh-MIME-us

Gallimimus had a beak rather than jaws.
It used the beak to chop up lizards,
eggs, insects, and plants before
swallowing. It used its three-clawed
hands for digging up insects and roots.

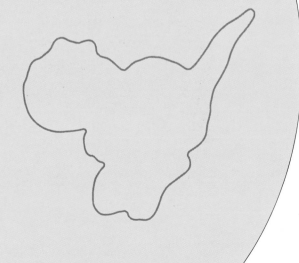

Dromiceiomimus

DROH-mee-see-uh-MIME-us

Dromiceiomimus was possibly the first
raptor. Like all raptors, it had a slashing
claw on the second toe of each foot.

Elmisaurus

ELM-ee-SAWR-us

Elmisaurus had very thin,
light bones. Its skeleton,
therefore, did not weigh
very much, which made it
a very fast runner.

▶UP CLOSE: **Gallimimus**

Gallimimus was an ornithomimosaur, a group also known as "ostrich dinosaurs." These animals had very long, strong hind legs; long, thin necks; and a small head.

Its flattened, toothless jaws were edged with a horn, forming a beak.

Gallimimus ate plants, small mammals and reptiles, large insects, and eggs.

! **FACT-TASTIC**
Gallimimus became famous in 1993 when a stampeding herd of the creatures appeared in the movie Jurassic Park.

Like ostriches, Gallimimus could run very fast, and probably evaded predators simply by outrunning them.

The
...atory
...nosaurs

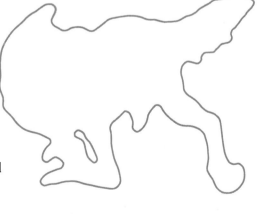

Garudimimus

ga-ROOD-uh-MIME-us
Garudimimus was an
omnivore—it ate both
plants and animals. It had
no teeth, so it would cut
up its food with its beak
and swallow it whole.

Harpymimus

HAR-pee-MIME-us
Harpymimus had its eyes set on the sides
of its head. It would have been able to
see all around itself, but would have had
to turn its head to look to the front.

Mononykus

mo-NON-i-kus
Mononykus was covered
with feathers, which would
have provided protection
against the winter cold or
nighttime temperatures.

▶UP CLOSE: **Mononykus**

Mononykus was a bizarre-looking theropod. It was tiny, less than three feet long and weighing less than six pounds. It lived on the dry, dusty plains of Mongolia 67 million years ago, making it one of the last dinosaurs.

Mononykus had a very birdlike head with a toothless beak, and huge eyes to spot fast-moving lizards and insects.

Mononykus was probably covered in hairy feathers, which would have helped it keep warm. There is no way to know what color these feathers would have been.

Its arms were very short but powerful. At the end of each was a single, large, banana-shaped claw. It probably used its claws for ripping into termite nests, and then it gulped the insects up with its tongue.

❗ FACT-TASTIC
Experts believe that Mononykus actually evolved from an ancient flying bird, but lost the use of its wings.

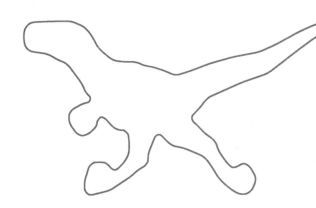

Noasaurus

NOH-ah-SAWR-us

An adult Noasaurus could grow up to eight feet in height. Hunting as a pack, several of these creatures could bring down a large, plant-eating dinosaur.

Oviraptor

OH-vi-RAP-tor

Oviraptor means "egg robber." Paleontologists first thought the dinosaur lived mainly on eggs, but they now believe it also ate lizards, insects, and plants.

 **FACT-TASTIC**

Oviraptor's curious crest may have been used for display, for cooling its brain, or to help it make loud calls.

Pelicanimimus

PEL-uh-kan-uh-MIME-us

Pelicanimimus had a deep pouch beneath its lower jaw, like a pelican's. It may have waded into lakes, caught fish, and stored the fish in the pouch to feed to its young later.

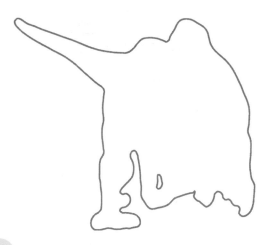

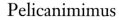

Saurornithoides

SAWR-or-NITH-oy-dees

Saurornithoides had its eyes on the front of its head rather than at the sides. It could judge distance very well, which made it a skillful hunter of small prey.

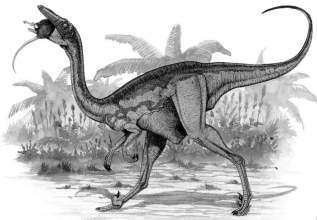

Troödon

TROH-oh-don

Troödon had teeth that were sharpened just on one side, like steak knives. The shape of the teeth allowed it to slice through the toughest skin.

Struthiomimus

STROOTH-ee-o-MIME-us

Struthiomimus ran extremely fast to catch its prey, holding its long tail out straight behind it for balance. It also ate plants and eggs.

▶UP CLOSE: **Troödon**

Troödon was a small, birdlike theropod that lived in North America around 70 million years ago. Like others of its kind, it had long hind legs with a sickle-shaped claw on the second toe, and a birdlike skull. It had a large brain and was probably one of the smartest of all dinosaurs.

With its eyes set forward on its head like a bird of prey's, Troödon could hunt with great accuracy in dim light or at night.

A long, whiplike tail was perfect for balance when running.

Strong hind legs allowed a pack of hunting Troödons to chase down small prey.

 FACT-TASTIC

Troödon dug a round nest in the ground and laid about 24 eggs. The mother incubated the eggs, just like birds do today.

Did you know?
Utahraptor was one of the fiercest of all meat-eating dinosaurs and could grow to more than 20 feet in length.

Velociraptor
va-LOSS-ah-RAP-tor
Velociraptor grew to seven feet in length and was armed with knifelike teeth and two slashing talons.

Utahraptor
YOO-tah-RAP-tor
Utahraptor could deliver a powerful kick with its hind legs and could also attack its prey with retractable toe talons that were over a foot long.

Ankylosaurs

The ankylosaurs were the most armored of all the dinosaurs. To protect themselves from predators, they had thick, bony plates, or scutes, embedded in the skin across their backs, tails, and heads. Some even had armored eyelids! Their bodies were very wide and heavy and their legs were short, which made them almost impossible to tip over. This meant that predators could not easily attack their softer bellies.

All ankylosaurs were plant-eaters. Scientists think that they probably fermented their food in their guts to make it more digestible, like rhinos and elephants do today. Ankylosaurs can be divided into two main groups: some, like Edmontonia, had large spikes extending from the shoulders; others had smaller spikes on their shoulders but had a massive, bony club at the end of their tails, which could be swung at attackers like a hammer.

Although most ankylosaurs were large and walked on all fours, some early species were much smaller and could probably walk on either two or four legs. Ankylosaurs originated in the middle of the Jurassic period, but became more widespread during the Cretaceous.

Ankylosaurs

Ankylosaurus

ang-KY-loh-SAWR-us

Ankylosaurus was built like a tank! Its head and back were covered with bony plates and long spikes, and it had a vicious bone club at the end of its tail.

! FACT-TASTIC

Ankylosaurus's head was almost three feet long. It was so thick and bony that there was very little room for a brain!

Did you know?

Pisanosaurus was discovered in northern Argentina. It is the earliest known plant-eating dinosaur, dating from the Triassic period.

Pisanosaurus

pie-ZAHN-oh-SAWR-us

An early ankylosaur, Pisanosaurus was tiny, reaching only three feet in length and a foot in height.

Dracopelta

drack-oh-PELL-ta

If it was attacked, Dracopelta could rely on its bony covering and sharp body spikes for protection. It would grip the ground with its claws to keep itself from being flipped over.

Emausaurus

EE-mau-SAWR-us

Emausaurus had leaf-shaped teeth—it used these to pull off large amounts of leaves from branches. Much of its body was covered in bony scales.

Edmontonia

ed-mon-TOE-nee-ah

Edmontonia had two huge spines on each shoulder. One pointed forward to protect the head and neck; the other pointed backward to protect the sides.

Euoplocephalus

YOU-oh-plo-SEF-ah-lus

Euoplocephalus was covered in scutes and had a crushing tail club that weighed more than 30 pounds.

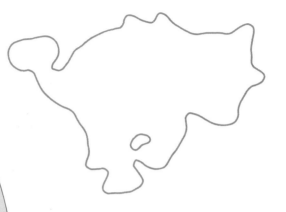

Minmi

MIN-mee

Minmi was discovered in Queensland, Australia. This small, armored dinosaur is named after Minmi Crossing, where it was found.

Hylaeosaurus

hi-LEE-oh-SAWR-us

Hylaeosaurus could weigh up to a ton and was heavily armored with bony plates and spikes. It had a toothless beak and ate low-lying plants such as ferns.

▶UP CLOSE: **Euoplocephalus**

At around 26 feet long, Euoplocephalus was one of the largest of all the ankylosaurs. It had short, powerful legs and weighed nearly four tons.

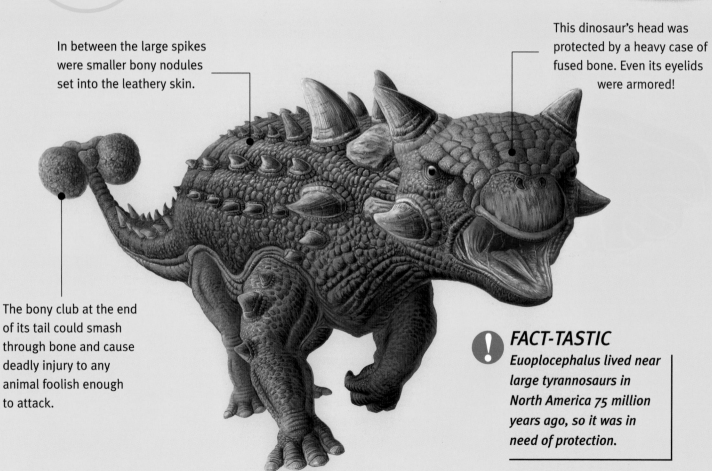

In between the large spikes were smaller bony nodules set into the leathery skin.

This dinosaur's head was protected by a heavy case of fused bone. Even its eyelids were armored!

The bony club at the end of its tail could smash through bone and cause deadly injury to any animal foolish enough to attack.

❗ FACT-TASTIC
Euoplocephalus lived near large tyrannosaurs in North America 75 million years ago, so it was in need of protection.

Ankylosaurs

Nodosaurus
NODE-oh-SAWR-us
Nodosaurus means "knobbly lizard." It was given the name because of its hard shell of knob-covered bony plates. We do not know if it also had spikes.

Panoplosaurus
PAN-oh-ploh-SAWR-us
Like most ankylosaurs, Panoplosaurus had a toothless beak for feeding on low plants. It was a massive animal, weighing up to three and a half tons.

Did you know?
Ankylosaurs were common at the end of the dinosaur era, around 65 million years ago. Ankylosaur fossils have even been found in Antarctica.

Pinacosaurus
PIN-ah-co-SAWR-us
Paleontologists recently found 20 fossilized skeletons of young Pinacosauruses in one place. This discovery could mean that the herd was divided into groups by age.

Polacanthus

pole-ah-CAN-thus

Polacanthus weighed around a ton. It had four pillarlike legs to support its weight, but it would have moved very slowly.

Scelidosaurus

SKEL-eye-doh-SAWR-us

Scelidosaurus means "limb lizard," a reference to the dinosaur's strong hind legs. It lived around 200 million years ago.

Saichania

siy-KAHN-ee-ah

Saichania had an excellent sense of smell, which was used to detect both predators and food. It also used its large nasal cavity to increase the volume of its deafening roar.

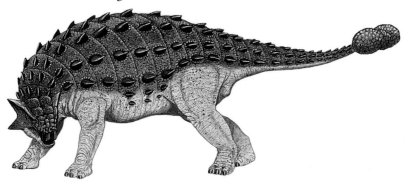

▶UP CLOSE: **Scelidosaurus**

Scelidosaurus was a small, armored dinosaur that lived in Europe around 200 million years ago. It is not a true ankylosaur, but it was from animals such as this that the ankylosaurs evolved.

! FACT-TASTIC
Sir Richard Owen, who named Scelidosaurus, also coined the word "dinosaur" in 1842. It means "terrible lizard."

Scelidosaurus shared its environment with a number of larger predators, but its armor would have made it a difficult meal.

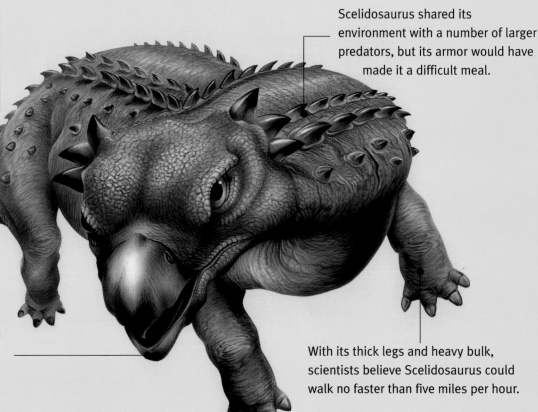

Scelidosaurus ate low-growing ferns, which were bitten off with its strong beak and crushed with its small, spoon-shaped teeth. It could not chew its food.

With its thick legs and heavy bulk, scientists believe Scelidosaurus could walk no faster than five miles per hour.

Silvisaurus

SILL-vah-SAWR-us

Silvisaurus was a type of dinosaur known as a nodosaur. Nodosaurs did not have a tail club like many other ankylosaurs.

Struthiosaurus

STROO-thee-oh-SAWR-us

Struthiosaurus is the smallest armored dinosaur known. An adult measured about six feet long from head to tail.

Talarurus

TAL-a-RU-rus

Most predators would avoid trying to eat a Talarurus. Not only would it be difficult to bite through its bony plates, but the tail club was capable of smashing even thick dinosaur bones.

Stegosaurs

Stegosaurs are a well-known group of dinosaurs, and some of them looked very bizarre, with a heavy body, a small head, long hind legs, and large plates sticking straight up from their backs. Indeed, their name means "roof reptile," because the large plates on their backs resemble roof tiles.

However, most stegosaurs didn't have plates on their backs. Among the few that did is the famous Stegosaurus itself. Other stegosaurs had long spikes instead of plates running along their backs and their tails. The tip of the tail had long spikes, which were used for defense against predatory dinosaurs.

Stegosaurs were plant-eaters. They had rather feeble teeth in their long, narrow heads, and their forelimbs were much shorter than their hind limbs, which brought the head close to the ground. Scientists think that they mainly fed on soft, low-growing ferns, which were very common in the Jurassic period.

Stegosaurs had their heyday in the Jurassic, and only a few survived into the Cretaceous period. Scientists are still not sure why they became extinct, but they believe that the increased competition from other plant-eating dinosaurs may have proved to be too much for the stegosaurs.

Stegosaurs

Chailingosaurus
CHEE-ah-LING-ah-SAWR-us
Chailingosaurus was a plant-eating dinosaur with an extremely small brain. Based on skull fossils, paleontologists have calculated its brain as the size of a golf ball.

Dravidosaurus
druh-VID-oh-SAWR-us
Some paleontologists believe that Dravidosaurus actually lived in the water. Others argue that the plates on its back aren't typical of a marine dinosaur.

Dacentrurus
dah-sen-TROO-rus
Dacentrurus had two rows of plates and spikes along its back and tail for defense. Some of these spikes could be 17 inches long.

Did you know?
For many years it was believed that stegosaurs had a second brain in their tails that was responsible for controlling their hindquarters.

Huayangosaurus

hwah-YANG-oh-SAWR-us

Huayangosaurus had a set of small teeth that was used for stripping leaves off branches. Later species similar to Huayangosaurus simply had toothless beaks.

Kentrosaurus

KEN-troh-SAWR-us

Kentrosaurus had plates and spikes along its back and tail, and two more spikes jutting out from the hips. The hip spikes protected the dinosaur's sides from attack.

Lexovisaurus

lek-SOH-vee-SAWR-us

The spikes on Lexovisaurus's body were used for more than just defense. They would also help attract mates and kept the animal cool by absorbing the heat of the sun.

103

Stegosaurs

Stegosaurus

STEG-o-SAWR-us

Stegosaurus had a total of 17 bony plates along its back. If attacked, the dinosaur would swing its highly dangerous spiked tail at the enemy.

! FACT-TASTIC

Scientists believe that some stegosaurs' plates were covered in skin and could change color to attract a mate.

Wuerhosaurus

woo-AYR-hoh-SAWR-us

Wuerhosaurus was the last of the stegosaurs. Although it had good protection on its back and tail, its open sides were exposed to a predator's bite.

▶UP CLOSE: **Stegosaurus**

Stegosaurus is the most famous of all the stegosaurs—and it was also the largest. It could reach a length of 30 feet and weighed three tons.

❗ FACT-TASTIC

A Stegosaurus's tiny brain probably weighed less than a thousandth of the animal's total body weight.

Stegosaurus's head was tiny in relation to its body. It contained small, weak teeth for eating soft plants.

All along its back were huge plates, which could be over three feet long.

The tip of the tail bore four long, pointed spikes, two on each side. Stegosaurus would have used these to lash out at predators.

Forest clearing

Millions of years ago, Hypsilophodon and Iguanodon would nibble at leaves in this forest clearing while watching out for Deinonychus and Troödon, who could attack without warning. Create your own forest scene with your dinosaur stickers.

Iguanodonts and Duckbills

The iguanodonts were a very successful group of plant-eating dinosaurs.
They lived in the Jurassic and Cretaceous periods, and were found across much
of the planet. Some of them were no larger than a turkey, but others, such as the
famous Iguanodon itself, weighed as much as a small elephant.

The iguanodonts could chew their food, which was unusual for plant-eating dinosaurs.
They had large teeth and probably ate both soft and coarse plants. Although their
forelimbs were always much shorter than their hind limbs, scientists think that only the
smaller species walked around using just their hind limbs. The large species were
probably so heavy that they had to walk on all fours.

In the Cretaceous period, the iguanodonts gave rise to the duck-billed dinosaurs. These
creatures had wide muzzles, and it was once thought that they lived in swamps and used
their muzzles to skim the water for aquatic plants, the way ducks do today. But now we
know that they lived on dry land and roamed about in large herds. They used their wide
beaks for cropping off plant leaves, which they chewed with hundreds of grinding teeth.

Iguanodonts and Duckbills

Abrictosaurus

uh-BRICK-tuh-SAWR-us

Abrictosaurus was a plant-eating animal that lived in southern Africa. Some paleontologists think it may have hibernated during the African dry season.

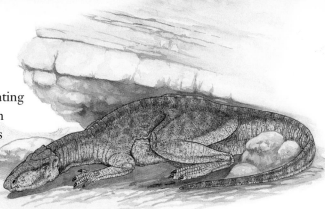

FACT-TASTIC

A complete Anatotitan skeleton, more than 36 feet long, is on display at the American Museum of Natural History in New York.

Did you know?
Aralosaurus fossils were discovered on the shores of the Aral Sea in Kazakhstan, in central Asia, when the sea began to dry up.

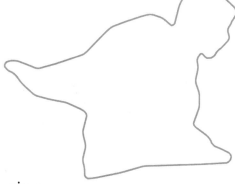

Anatotitan

ah-NAT-uh-TIE-tan

Anatotitan means "giant duck." The dinosaur had a mouth shaped like a duck's beak, and it contained 720 teeth for grinding up plant food.

Aralosaurus

AR-a-lo-SAWR-us

Aralosaurus had loose skin on its nose, which it could inflate with air in order to make a very loud bellow.

Atlascoposaurus

AT-las-KOP-kuh-SAWR-us

Atlascoposaurus was a sprinting dinosaur. If it spotted a predator, it would run away at high speed, making quick turns to evade its attacker.

Brachylophosaurus

BRACK-uh-LOF-o-SAWR-us

A complete Brachylophosaurus skeleton was found in 2000. It was trapped in a sand bank and had been mummified. Its stomach contained fossilized ferns, conifers, and flowers.

Camptosaurus

KAMP-toe-SAWR-us

Camptosaurus stood on four legs to feed on grasses and low-lying plants, but it could also stand on just its hind legs to eat leaves from taller trees.

Dryosaurus

DRY-oh-SAWR-us

Dryosauruses lived together in large herds. The herds provided safety— more pairs of keen eyes were available to look out for predators.

Corythosaurus

co-RITH-oh-SAWR-us

Corythosaurus had a large, hollow, bony crest on top of its head. The crest actually held parts of the animal's brain linked to its sense of smell.

Gilmoreosaurus

GIL-mohr-o-SAWR-us
Gilmoreosaurus generally walked on all fours, but could rise and run on its muscular hind legs if it was in danger.

Fulgurotherium

FULL-gur-oh-THEER-ee-um
Fulgurotherium lived in Australia at a time when the continent was actually within the Antarctic Circle. The dinosaur would migrate to avoid the coldest weather.

 FACT-TASTIC

Dinosaurs suffered from disease, just like humans. Fossils of Gilmoreosaurus show cancerous growths in their tails.

Iguanodonts and Duckbills

Hypsilophodon

hip-seh-LOFF-oh-don

When Hypsilophodon opened and closed its mouth, its teeth rubbed against each other. The rubbing action caused the teeth to become sharper.

Hadrosaurus

HAD-roh-SAWR-us

Hadrosaurus was the first nearly complete fossilized dinosaur skeleton to go on public display. Found in the northeastern United States, it was assembled and shown in 1868.

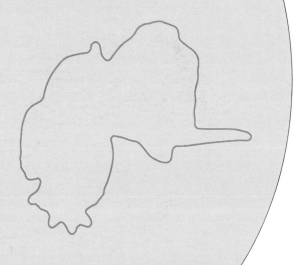

Hypacrosaurus

hi-PACK-roe-SAWR-us

Hypacrosaurus had a total of 40 rows of teeth in its mouth! With these, it ground up every type of plant material, from pine needles to fruit.

▶UP CLOSE: Hypsilophodon

Hypsilophodon was a slender, plant-eating dinosaur that could dash around on its long hind limbs. It lived in Europe 120 million years ago.

Hypsilophodon was so small and athletic that it could outrun most of its enemies, which included the early tyrannosaur Eotyrannus.

Hypsilophodon could chew tough plant food with a circular movement of its lower jaw. It also had a fleshy cheek, so the food did not drop out of its mouth when it chewed.

Its muscular thighs and five-toed feet gave it the legs of a sprinter.

❗ FACT-TASTIC

When it was first discovered, experts thought that Hypsilophodon was a young Iguanodon.

▶UP CLOSE: **Iguanodon**

Iguanodon was common throughout Europe 110 to 130 million years ago. It was a very large plant-eater, up to 30 feet long and weighing three tons.

! *FACT-TASTIC*

Iguanodon was found before the word "dinosaur" had been coined. Its name means "iguana tooth."

Its sharp, toothless beak was used to nip off tasty leaves and buds, which would be ground up by teeth at the back of the mouth.

Scientists now believe that Iguanodon walked on all fours with its tail stretched out behind it, rather than upright like a kangaroo.

On each of Iguanodon's thumbs was a huge spike, which was probably used for defense.

Iguanodon

ig-WAHN-oh-don

Iguanodon had a sharp thumb spike on its five-fingered hands. The spike was between two and six inches long and provided a formidable defense against predators.

Jaxartosaurus

jack-SAHR-toh-SAWR-us

Jaxartosaurus made an extremely loud trumpeting noise using its throat and nostrils. It used the sound to attract mates and to scare away predators.

Lambeosaurus

LAM-bee-oh-SAWR-us

Lambeosaurus was named after Lawrence Lambe, a Canadian fossil hunter. It was the largest of the duck-billed dinosaurs.

Leaellynasaura

lee-EL-in-a-SAWR-ah

Female Leaellynasauras would lay their eggs in a nest dug into the ground. They would guard the nest and keep the eggs warm until the young were hatched.

Maiasaura

MY-yah-SAWR-ah

In an incredible find in the western United States, around 10,000 Maiasaura fossils and 40 nests were discovered. The find proved that Maiasaura was a herding animal.

Mandschurosaurus

mand-CHOOR-o-SAWR-us

Paleontologists at first thought that Mandschurosaurus had webbed feet and was a swimming animal. However, we now know that Mandschurosaurus was a land-living plant-eater.

▶UP CLOSE: Maiasaura

Maiasaura means "good mother lizard." And a good mother it was! Scientists have found many Maiasaura nests, often with small baby Maiasaura fossils inside them. The adults would bring plant food back to the infants, just like birds do today.

The long spine was stiffened with bony tendons that helped support its tail, which was used for balance.

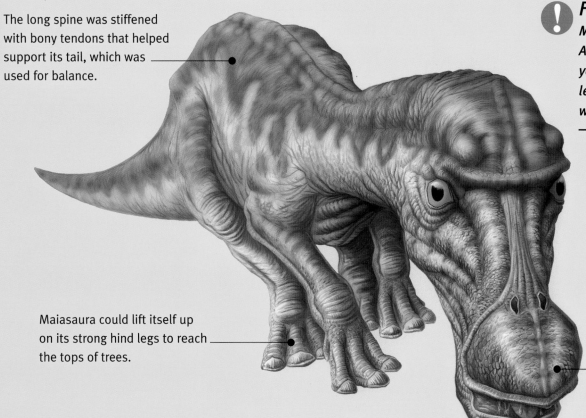

! **FACT-TASTIC**
Maiasaura lived in North America around 75 million years ago. It reached a length of 30 feet and weighed up to three tons.

Maiasaura could lift itself up on its strong hind legs to reach the tops of trees.

Its wide, toothless beak was ideal for cropping off plants, which were chewed by hundreds of small teeth farther back in the jaw.

Muttaburrasaurus

mutt-ah-BUHR-ah-SAWR-us

Muttaburrasaurus had very wide feet with hooflike claws. These feet allowed the dinosaur to walk over soft ground without sinking in.

Nipponosaurus

ni-PON-oh-SAWR-us

Nipponosaurus had a special crest on its head. It would use this crest like an echo chamber to make extremely loud calls that could be heard far away.

Othnielia

OTH-ni-EE-lee-ah

Othnielia had very small teeth and jaws. It was only able to eat soft plant foods, such as flowers and leaves.

! **FACT-TASTIC**

Nipponosaurus ("Japan lizard") got its name from Russia's Sakhalin Island, which was a part of Japan when it was discovered.

Ouranosaurus

oo-RAHN-oh-SAWR-us

Ouranosaurus had a sail on its back for controlling its body temperature. The sail released body heat when the dinosaur was warm and pulled in heat from the sun when the dinosaur was cold.

Parksosaurus

PARK-soh-SAWR-us

Parksosaurus was a small, plant-eating dinosaur. It grew up to seven feet in length and weighed around 230 pounds when it was fully grown.

Parasaurolophus

PAIR-uh-SOAR-uh-LOAF-us

Of all the duck-billed dinosaurs, Parasaurolophus had the longest crest on its head. It was a large creature, standing around 16 feet tall.

▶UP CLOSE: **Parasaurolophus**

Parasaurolophus was a large duck-billed dinosaur that lived in North America 70 to 75 million years ago. Like most duckbills, it mainly moved around on all fours and fed on low-lying plants and shrubs.

! *FACT-TASTIC*

Different species of Parasaurolophus have different sizes and shapes of crests, suggesting each made a particular note.

On the back of its head, Parasaurolophus had an enormous, three-foot-long crest. The crest was hollow and connected to the nose. By blowing into it, the animal could make a deafening noise!

Like a rhinoceros, Parasaurolophus had broad, three-toed hind feet to support its huge weight.

The forefeet were smaller than the hind feet but had four toes. They would have been used for digging but would not have been much use for defense.

Saurolophus

SAWR-oh-LOAF-us

Saurolophus had no teeth in the front of its jaws. When eating, it used hundreds of teeth in its cheeks to mash the food so it could be swallowed.

Prosaurolophus

PRO-sore-o-LOAF-us

The crest of Prosaurolophus's nose acted like a "resonating chamber"—a cavity used to increase the volume of its roars and bellows.

Rhabdodon

RAB-doe-don

Rhabdodon had five-fingered hands. The hands were ideal for grabbing hold of plants and bending them over into the mouth when feeding.

Iguanodonts and Duckbills

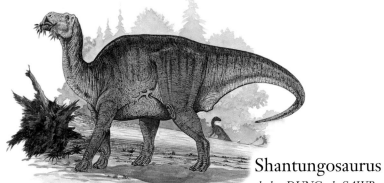

Shantungosaurus
shahn-DUNG-oh-SAWR-us
Shantungosaurus lived around the coasts and rivers of China some 80 million years ago. It was a heavy dinosaur, weighing up to seven tons, but could run quickly.

Did you know?
Shantungosaurus is the largest plant-eating duck-billed dinosaur ever discovered. It was even larger than Tyrannosaurus rex.

Secernosaurus
see-SIR-no-SAWR-us
The fossilized skeleton of a Secernosaurus was found in Argentina in 1932. It wasn't until 1979, however, that the dinosaur was identified.

Tenontosaurus
ten-ONT-oh-SAWR-us
Tenontosaurus browsed for grasses and plants on all four legs, but ran on its hind legs when attacked or threatened.

Thescelosaurus

THES-ke-loh-SAWR-us

Scientists have recently discovered that Thescelosaurus was a warm-blooded animal, like modern birds, rather than cold-blooded, like modern reptiles.

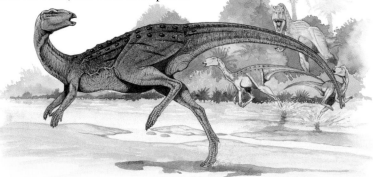

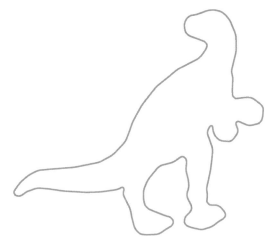

Xiaosaurus

sheow-SAWR-us

Xiaosaurus was only five feet long, so it would make a good snack for a predator. Yet Xiaosaurus's good eyesight and fast reflexes made it difficult to catch.

Tsintaosaurus

sin-tau-SAWR-us

Tsintaosaurus had no body weapons to defend itself against predators. If attacked, it tried to scare off the attacker with a loud bellow—or it simply ran away.

Horned Dinosaurs

The horned dinosaurs are some of the most famous and striking dinosaurs ever to have lived. Most people will know a Triceratops as soon as they see it. However, not all horned dinosaurs were large and rhinoceros-like. The earliest ones, such as Psittacosaurus, were tiny and ran around on their long hind limbs, but they still had the characteristic beak and wide head of later species.

Scientists think that horned dinosaurs originated in Asia, as that is where the oldest fossils have been found. This is where they took the next step in their evolution, where they became larger and began walking on all fours. These animals, known as protoceratopsids, then spread to North America. Several protoceratopsids are featured in this chapter, including Protoceratops and Leptoceratops.

The horned dinosaurs thrived in North America. Here, they gradually evolved into the ceratopsids—the group that includes Triceratops. These were rhino- to elephant-sized animals, with strong bodies, short and muscular legs, and large heads with horns on the nose and over the eyes. So far, ceratopsids have been found only in North America.

The horned dinosaurs were plant-eaters, and many of them lived in large herds. This would have offered good protection against predatory dinosaurs.

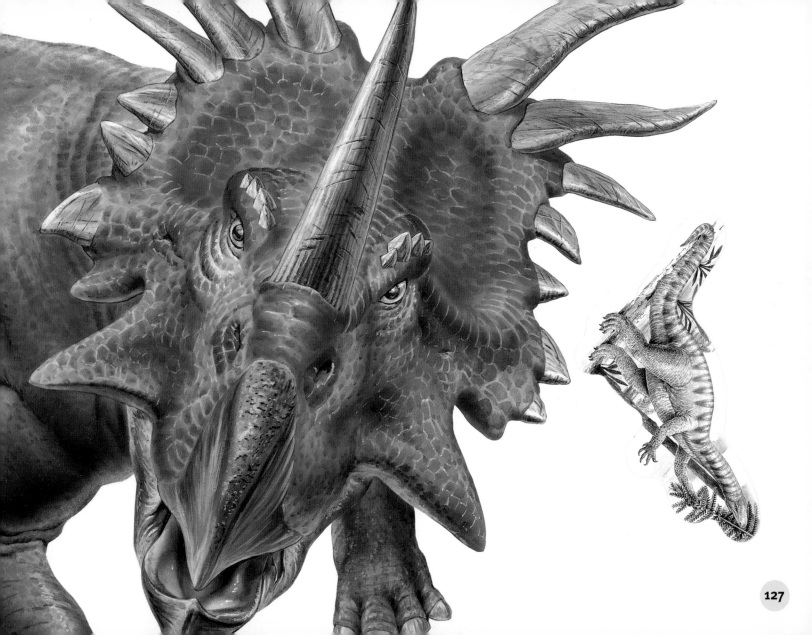

Horned Dinosaurs

Anchiceratops

AN-key-SAIR-ah-tops

Anchiceratops had a large neck frill to protect its neck from the bite of a predator. It was too heavy to be made of solid bone, so it had two holes to make it lighter.

Arrhinoceratops

aye-RYE-no-SAIR-uh-tops

Like most of the horned dinosaurs, Arrhinoceratops had a large neck frill with two holes in the bone. The holes were covered with skin, so the frill looked solid.

Avaceratops

AY-vah-SAIR-uh-tops

Avaceratops had a sharp, toothless beak. It would shear off large pieces of plants, which it then chewed using its rear teeth.

Did you know?
An Avaceratops fossil was found in 1981 by two amateur paleontologists, Ed and Ava Cole. The species was named after Ava.

Bagaceratops
BAG-uh-SAIR-uh-tops
Bagaceratops was a small dinosaur that grew to around 40 inches in length. It lived in groups and made nests in sand dunes.

Brachyceratops
BRACK-ee-SAIR-uh-tops
Only fossils of young Brachyceratops have been found, so we don't know for sure what the adults looked like.

Centrosaurus
SEN-tro-SAWR-us
Centrosaurus was a massive plant-eating dinosaur that weighed up to 13 tons. Its large nose horn was 18 inches long and was a powerful weapon.

▶UP CLOSE: **Centrosaurus**

Centrosaurus was a very common horned dinosaur that lived in North America around 75 million years ago. It was the size of a rhino and bore a large, slightly curved horn on its nose.

Like other ceratopsians, Centrosaurus had a bulky body—it weighed in at around three tons.

Centrosaurus's horn was used to fight with other centrosaurs, and also to ward off predators such as tyrannosaurs.

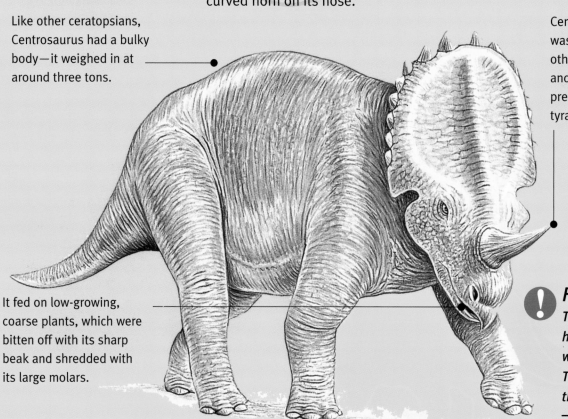

It fed on low-growing, coarse plants, which were bitten off with its sharp beak and shredded with its large molars.

! **FACT-TASTIC**

The remains of a huge herd of Centrosauruses were found in Canada. The herd contained more than 10,000 individuals!

Chasmosaurus
KAS-mo-SAWR-us
Chasmosaurus had a huge neck shield. However, it was not strong enough to provide much protection and simply made the dinosaur look bigger.

Einiosaurus
eye-nee-oh-SAWR-us
Einiosaurus was a strange-looking dinosaur. It had two straight horns on its neck frill and a single, downward-curving horn on its nose. These horns were more scary than dangerous.

Diceratops
die-SAIR-uh-tops
Diceratops weighed around 11 tons. It was so heavy that it could only walk at a speed of about two miles per hour.

131

Horned Dinosaurs

Leptoceratops
LEP-to-SAIR-uh-tops
Leptoceratops's body was very vulnerable to predators, although it could run reasonably quickly and could give a bone-breaking bite with its strong beak.

Microceratops
MY-cro-SAIR-uh-tops
Microceratops means "tiny horned face." The creature was the smallest of the horned dinosaurs, and grew to only two feet long.

❗ FACT-TASTIC
Nests of fossilized Montanoceratops have been discovered. Each nest contained 12 eggs laid in a spiral pattern.

Montanoceratops
mon-TAN-oh-SAIR-uh-tops
Montanoceratops lived in large herds in what is now Montana. It laid its eggs in nesting grounds shared by other members of the herd.

Pachyrhinosaurus

pack-ee-RINE-oh-SAWR-us

A discovery of hundreds of Pachyrhinosaurus bones in Canada shows that these creatures lived in herds.

Protoceratops

PRO-toh-SAIR-uh-tops

A famous fossil site revealed the bones of Protoceratops in battle with the predator Velociraptor. Both dinosaurs had been killed during the fight by a falling sand dune.

Pentaceratops

PEN-ta-SAIR-uh-tops

Pentaceratops had an awesome neck frill that could grow up to 10 feet in length. The huge frill, which was studded with spikes, was used to frighten off predators.

▶UP CLOSE: **Protoceratops**

Protoceratops was a primitive horned dinosaur known as a protoceratopsid. It lived on the dry plains of Asia around 80 million years ago. Protoceratops lived in small herds and fed on low-growing shrubs.

! *FACT-TASTIC*

This strange beast with its remarkable neck frill seems to have lived like modern-day sheep, in grazing herds.

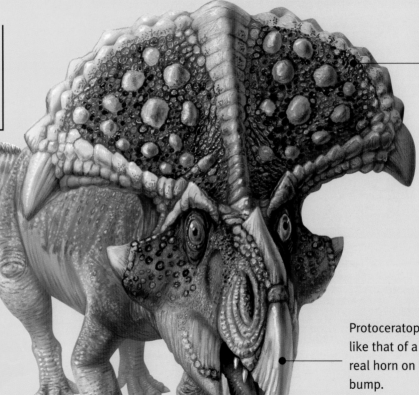

The neck frill was supported by struts of bone rather than solid bone. It was probably used more to impress a mate than for defense.

The long tail indicates that Protoceratops evolved from dinosaurs that walked on two legs. They needed this long tail for balance.

Protoceratops had a horny beak like that of a bird. It did not have a real horn on its nose, just a small bump.

Psittacosaurus

SIT-ah-co-SAWR-us

Psittacosaurus had a beak like that of a parrot. It also had very long claws for digging up roots to eat.

Styracosaurus

sty-RACK-oh-SAWR-us

The horn on Styracosaurus's nose grew up to two feet long and was six inches thick. It could attack a predator with this horn by charging it at up to 20 miles per hour.

Triceratops

tri-SAIR-uh-tops

Unlike other, similar dinosaurs, Triceratops's neck frill was made of solid bone. This made it a very heavy dinosaur, weighing up to seven tons.

▶UP CLOSE: **Psittacosaurus**

Psittacosaurus was a primitive horned dinosaur that lived in Asia 110 to 130 million years ago. It weighed just 30 to 40 pounds—tiny when compared to most other horned dinosaurs.

Some scientists think that Psittacosaurus was camouflaged to protect it from dangerous predators.

Psittacosaurus lacked the horns and frill of other horned dinosaurs, but it did have the characteristic beak, which was used for cropping plants.

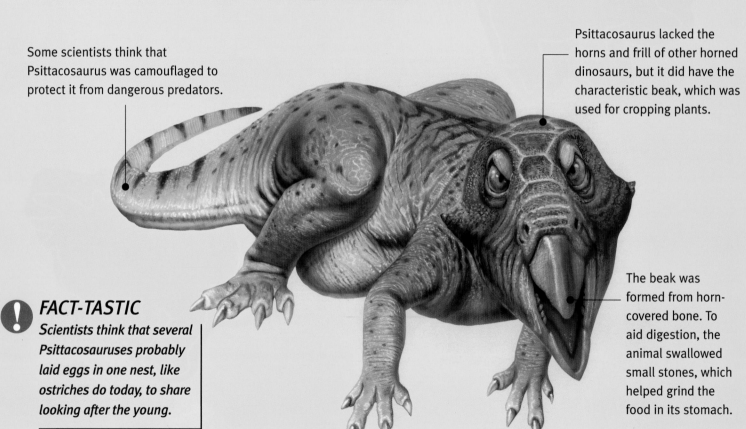

! FACT-TASTIC
Scientists think that several Psittacosauruses probably laid eggs in one nest, like ostriches do today, to share looking after the young.

The beak was formed from horn-covered bone. To aid digestion, the animal swallowed small stones, which helped grind the food in its stomach.

▶UP CLOSE: Triceratops

Triceratops was the largest of all the horned dinosaurs. It was a powerful animal that roamed in herds on the open plains of North America 65 to 67 million years ago.

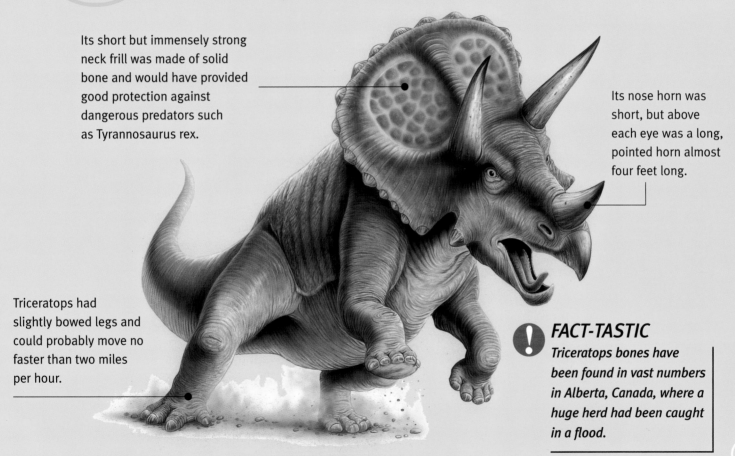

Its short but immensely strong neck frill was made of solid bone and would have provided good protection against dangerous predators such as Tyrannosaurus rex.

Its nose horn was short, but above each eye was a long, pointed horn almost four feet long.

Triceratops had slightly bowed legs and could probably move no faster than two miles per hour.

! FACT-TASTIC

Triceratops bones have been found in vast numbers in Alberta, Canada, where a huge herd had been caught in a flood.

Thick-headed Dinosaurs

The thick-headed dinosaurs were a group of small, plant-eating dinosaurs that lived in the Cretaceous period. They were never particularly numerous, and were much less common than iguanodonts, duckbills, and horned dinosaurs. However, they were still a successful and widespread group, as indicated by the discovery of their fossils in Europe, North America, and across Asia.

They looked similar to iguanodonts, and like this group they ran around on their long hind legs, using their arms and small hands to grasp plants. Their bodies were heavier and plumper than those of iguanodonts, and scientists think that they could not run as fast. The real differences are found in the heads. These dinosaurs had very thick skulls, and many of them had a great dome on top of their head. This made the animals look as if they had large brains, but the dome was made of solid bone.

The domes were probably used when competing with other animals during the mating season. Scientists used to think that they butted heads, but now they believe that these dinosaurs probably rammed each other along the sides of the body.

Thick-headed Dinosaurs

Pachycephalosaurus
pack-ee-SEF-ah-low-SAWR-us
Pachycephalosaurus mainly ate plants, seeds, and fruit. Some new fossils have shown that it also had front teeth, so it might have eaten some meat as well.

Goyocephale
GOH-yoh-SEF-ah-lee
Goyocephale had a thick, bony skull. It used its skull in battles with other males, shoving it against the opponent's body.

Homalocephale
HOME-ah-low-SEF-ah-lee
Paleontologists used to think that Homalocephales butted heads with one another. We now know that their skulls weren't strong enough to withstand such impacts.

▶UP CLOSE: **Pachycephalosaurus**

Pachycephalosaurus was the largest of all the thick-headed dinosaurs. It lived in North America at the very end of the Cretaceous period, 65 to 67 million years ago.

❗ *FACT-TASTIC*

Modern-day sheep and deer, along with many other animals, butt heads with each other to gain dominance, just like Pachycephalosaurus did.

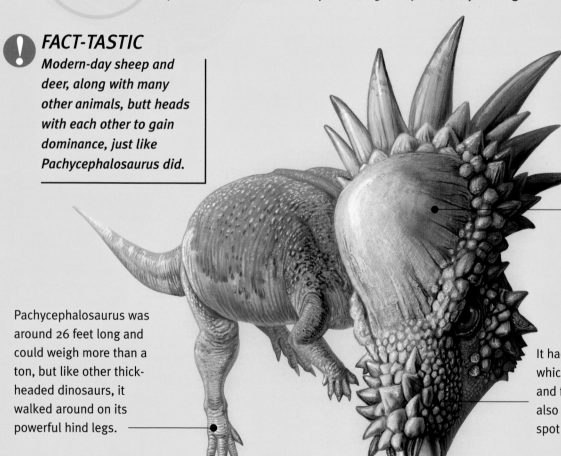

Pachycephalosaurus had an enormous, bony dome on top of its head—up to 10 inches thick! It probably used its head for ramming into other members of its own species during the mating season. But the massive dome would also have been an effective weapon against hungry predators.

Pachycephalosaurus was around 26 feet long and could weigh more than a ton, but like other thick-headed dinosaurs, it walked around on its powerful hind legs.

It had a very sensitive nose, which helped it sense danger and find food. Its eyes were also well developed, so it could spot predators.

Thick-headed Dinosaurs

Prenocephale

PREN-oh-SEF-ah-lee

Prenocephale had a large, bony dome on the top of its head. Its name actually means "sloping head." Fossils of this animal were found in Mongolia.

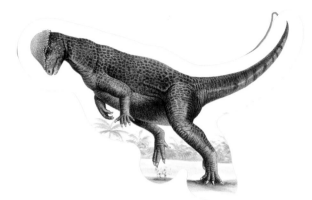

! FACT-TASTIC

The scary-looking Stygimoloch is named after the mythological river Styx and a mythical demon called Moloch.

Stygimoloch

STIJ-eh-MOLL-uk

Stygimoloch had clusters of sharp horns on top of its head. These weren't for fighting but for attracting females for mating.

Stenopelix

ste-NOP-uh-liks

Stenopelix had a beak full of blunt teeth. The teeth were not very good for chewing food, so Stenopelix swallowed small stones to help break down the food in its stomach.

Did you know?
Scientists believe that Stegocerases would have pressed their heads together like modern bulls, rather than butting, which would have caused too much damage.

Tylocephale
TIE-low-SEF-ah-lee
Of all the bone-headed dinosaurs, Tylocephale had the tallest skull. Its name means "swollen head."

Stegoceras
STEG-oh-CEER-us
Stegoceras had a bony dome on top of its skull that grew up to three inches thick. Male skulls were thicker than female skulls.

▶UP CLOSE: **Stegoceras**

Stegoceras lived in North America around 75 million years ago. Its skull dome was about three inches thick, and was thicker in males than in females.

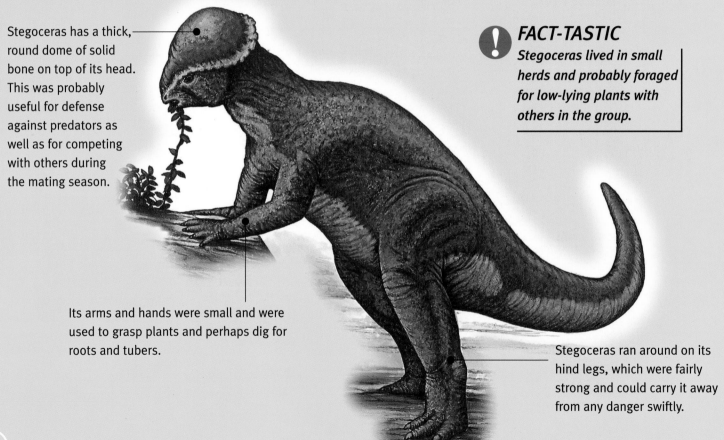

Stegoceras has a thick, round dome of solid bone on top of its head. This was probably useful for defense against predators as well as for competing with others during the mating season.

❗ FACT-TASTIC
Stegoceras lived in small herds and probably foraged for low-lying plants with others in the group.

Its arms and hands were small and were used to grasp plants and perhaps dig for roots and tubers.

Stegoceras ran around on its hind legs, which were fairly strong and could carry it away from any danger swiftly.

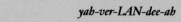

Wannanosaurus

wah-NAN-oh-SAWR-us

Wannanosaurus grew to just two feet long. It was constantly in danger of being eaten by larger predators such as Velociraptor.

Yaverlandia

yah-ver-LAN-dee-ah

Yaverlandia had two small domes on top of its skull. Males used these to shove other males around during fights over food or females.

❗ FACT-TASTIC

Yaverlandia was the first thick-headed dinosaur to be discovered outside North America.

Desert plain

Wide-open plains like this were usually home to large groups of dinosaurs struggling to survive in the harsh conditions. Centrosauruses would roam in herds looking for food while a Psittacosaurus would dig up roots with its beak. Create your own desert scene with your dinosaur stickers.

Flying Reptiles

The pterosaurs, or flying reptiles, were a very successful group of animals that lived alongside the dinosaurs. They were the first vertebrates, or animals with backbones, to take to the air, and from the end of the Triassic to the end of the Jurassic—a period of 70 million years—they ruled the skies. In the late Jurassic the birds appeared and the two groups lived alongside each other throughout the Cretaceous period.

The wings of pterosaurs were very different from those of both birds and bats. On bats, the leathery wing is stretched out across all five fingers of the hand, but on pterosaurs the fourth finger was enormously elongated; this finger carried the wing. The wing itself was different for each creature and consisted of several layers of skin. This made it strong, tough, and flexible, so the animals could maneuver easily in flight.

Pterosaurs had fur all over their bodies and were probably warm-blooded. Like other reptiles, they laid eggs and probably took care of their young. The more primitive species were about the same size as seagulls and had long tails. During the Cretaceous period, the pterosaurs lost their tails and several species grew to immense sizes. Some weighed more than a human being and had a wingspan of more than 30 feet—as much as that of a small airplane!

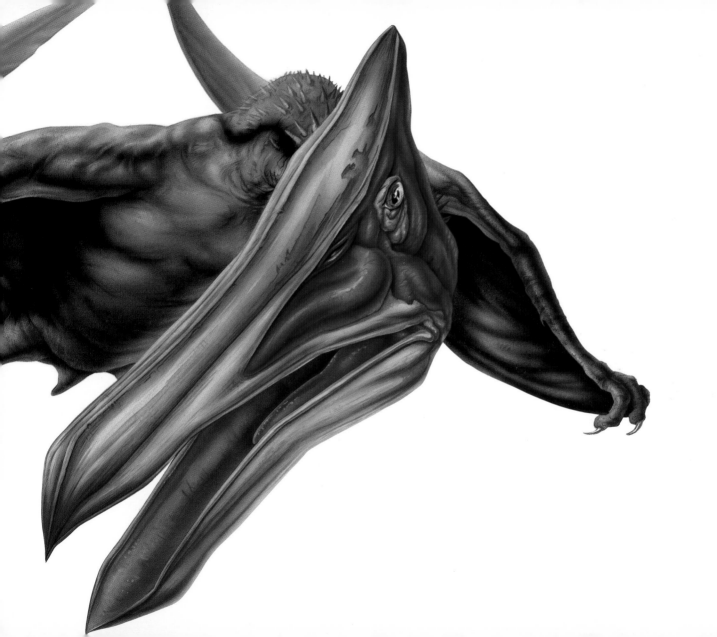

Flying Reptiles

Dsungaripterus
ZUN-ga-RIP-tare-us
Dsungaripterus had jaws that were long and thin and curved up at the end. They were ideal for prying shellfish off rocks.

Dimorphodon
die-MORE-foe-don
Dimorphodon's wings were thick and leathery. They were strengthened with thick fibers that worked like the struts of an umbrella.

Pteranodon
ter-AN-oh-don
Pteranodon had to flap its huge wings very hard to take off. Once it was airborne, however, it glided effortlessly on air currents.

▶UP CLOSE: **Pteranodon**

Pteranodon lived along the coasts of North America in the late Cretaceous period. At the back of the head was a large, hollow crest, which was probably used as a signal to other Pteranodons, similar to how modern birds use their colorful feathers.

Pteranodon would fly over the ocean hunting for fish and squid, which it snapped out of the water with its large, toothless beak.

Pteranodon was a huge animal. Some individuals had a wingspan of more than 23 feet.

Experts think that Pteranodon had oily, featherlike hair to keep it warm, but we cannot be certain just by looking at fossils.

! *FACT-TASTIC*
Huge pterosaurs had trouble taking off in still weather. They probably launched themselves off cliffs to get airborne.

Flying Reptiles

Quetzalcoatlus

KWET-zal-koh-AT-lus

Quetzalcoatlus was an enormous reptile that would tower over a human. Its body grew to 20 feet long and its wingspan was a massive 40 feet.

Pterodaustro

ter-oh-DAW-stroh

Pterodaustros lived in large groups. Some recent fossil finds show that they laid their eggs in communal nesting sites.

Tapejara

tah-pay-ZHAR-a

Tapejara had a crest on its head that could grow to 40 inches long. The male probably used this crest to attract females.

▶UP CLOSE: Pterodaustro

Pterodaustro was a bizarre-looking pterosaur. It appears to have dwelled inland instead of along the coasts, but probably lived near water.

! FACT-TASTIC

Pterosaurs may have been infested with parasites that sucked the blood from the fine blood vessels in their delicate wings.

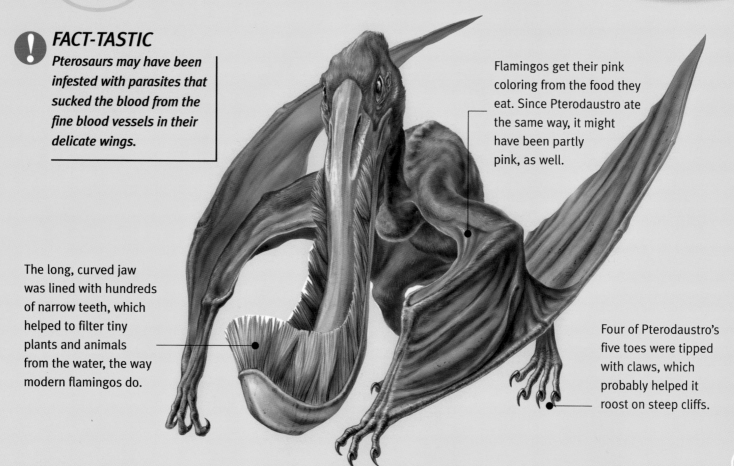

Flamingos get their pink coloring from the food they eat. Since Pterodaustro ate the same way, it might have been partly pink, as well.

The long, curved jaw was lined with hundreds of narrow teeth, which helped to filter tiny plants and animals from the water, the way modern flamingos do.

Four of Pterodaustro's five toes were tipped with claws, which probably helped it roost on steep cliffs.

153

Prehistoric Birds

Birds evolved from small, birdlike predatory dinosaurs sometime in the Jurassic period. Although most predatory dinosaurs lived on the ground, scientists are finding more evidence that some of them lived in the trees, climbing in the branches with their long arms and clawed hands.

Some small predators had feathers all over their bodies. Along their arms were particularly large feathers, and although they could not fly, they could use their long, feathered arms to glide short distances. Over time, the feathers on the arms grew longer and stiffer, and the animals began to flap their arms—so they could glide greater distances.

Fossils of small predatory dinosaurs from the late Jurassic period were so birdlike that scientists consider them to be more bird than dinosaur. These animals had very long arms lined with stiff flight feathers. They also had long feathers along the tail and fluffy feathers covering their bodies. They could fly by flapping their wings, like modern birds, but they were not very good at it.

These primitive birds eventually evolved into skilled fliers. Although modern-day birds may appear different from the creatures in this book, scientists classify them into the same group. This means that dinosaurs are not really extinct!

Hesperornis
HES-per-OR-nis
Hesperornis had a long, slim bill that was full of sharp teeth. It probably dived underwater to feed, grabbing squid and fish.

Archaeopteryx
ark-ee-OP-ter-icks
Archaeopteryx might have been the very first bird on earth. It couldn't fly very well, but it climbed up trees using strong claws on each wing.

▶UP CLOSE: Archaeopteryx

Archaeopteryx lived in Europe at the end of the Jurassic period, around 150 million years ago. It was about the size of a crow, and scientists regard it as the oldest known bird.

Archaeopteryx had fluffy feathers all over its body, strong, stiff flight feathers along its long arms, and long tail feathers.

Its skeleton looked remarkably similar to that of a small predatory dinosaur. It had the clawed hands and long, bony tail of a theropod.

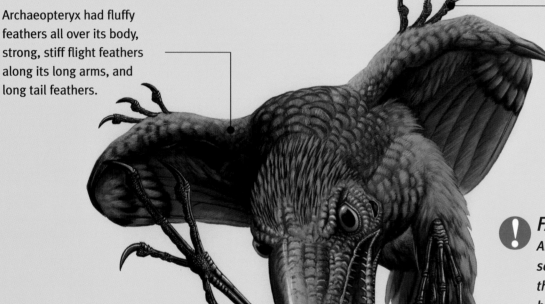

FACT-TASTIC

Archaeopteryx showed scientists the link between theropod dinosaurs and birds. Because of this, it has become one of the most famous fossils in the world.

Lined with sharp, pointed teeth, the jaws were like those of other meat-eating dinosaurs rather than the beaks of modern birds.

Diatryma

die-uh-TRY-mah

Diatryma grew up to seven feet tall and could not fly. It became extinct because its eggs, which were laid in nests on the ground, were eaten by other animals.

Argentavis

AR-jen-TAH-viss

Argentavis looked similar to a modern vulture. It was much bigger, however, with a wingspan of up to 25 feet!

Diatryma was a gigantic, ground-dwelling predatory bird that lived in North America around 50 million years ago. Much bigger than ostriches and emus, it stood over six feet tall and weighed nearly 300 pounds.

The stunted wings were not strong enough for flight but would have helped the bird balance when running fast.

Diatryma had a 10-inch-long beak, with which it would tear off large chunks of meat.

! FACT-TASTIC
Despite its large, ostrichlike size, Diatryma is more closely related to smaller cranes and herons.

With powerful four-toed feet tipped with sharp talons, Diatryma was a strong, fast-moving predator that preyed on the wide variety of medium-sized mammals that were common at the time.

Other Prehistoric Animals

Life on earth has taken on wild and wonderful forms throughout the ages. Most animal groups trace their origins to more than 500 million years ago, in a period known as the Precambrian. Scientists have found a myriad of strange and bizarre animals from this period in time, and some of them—including Hallucigenia and Anomalocaris—have no descendants today. Some of these Precambrian creatures are so odd that scientists are not sure which end is the head!

When dinosaurs roamed the land and pterosaurs soared in the skies, a wide variety of reptiles prowled the rivers, lakes, and seas throughout the world. They were not close relatives of the dinosaurs, but were closely related to today's lizards and snakes. Most of them fed on the dazzling variety of squid and fish that were common in the seas at the time. The most specialized of these marine reptiles, the ichthyosaurs, or whale-lizards, had large eyes, streamlined bodies, and could swim fast and dive to great depths. They even gave birth to live young, like modern whales and dolphins.

Other Prehistoric Animals

Ammonite
AM-uh-nite

Ammonites lived inside a hard spiral shell. The shell could be up to 10 feet in diameter and contained air to allow the ammonite to float underwater. It could squirt ink to deter predators.

Anomalocaris
ah-NOM-al-oh-KAR-is

Anomalocaris was swimming in the oceans 500 million years ago, well before dinosaurs walked on the land. It pushed itself through the water using fins.

Did you know?
Anomalocaris was the largest creature that lived in the Cambrian period. It was more than six feet long, and its name means "odd shrimp."

Arthropleura
AHR-throw-PLOOR-ah

Arthropleura crawled across forest floors, eating rotting vegetation. It had around 30 pairs of legs and breathed through little holes in its body.

Trilobite

TRY-low-bite

Trilobites lived on the seabeds. They are the earliest known animal with eyes, which were as solid as crystals.

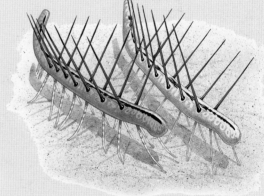

! FACT-TASTIC

Scientists originally thought Hallucigenia walked upside down, on its spikes. They still don't know which end was the head!

Pterygotus

TAIR-ee-GOAT-us

Pterygotus lived around 200 million years before the dinosaurs. Like a lobster, it had two pincers to catch and crush prey.

Hallucigenia

HAL-loo-see-GAIN-ee-ah

Hallucigenia scavenged for scraps of food on the bottom of the sea. It had seven spikes on each side of its body.

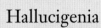

▶UP CLOSE: **Trilobite**

The trilobites were a very successful group of invertebrates (creatures without a backbone) that lived in the seas all over the world for hundreds of millions of years, from around 500 to 250 million years ago.

Trilobites were quite flat, with a distinctly segmented body, like modern-day insects and crustaceans. They are a distant ancestor of both.

The trilobite's antennae helped it locate food and sense danger in the darkness at the bottom of the sea.

On each of the trilobite's legs were feathery gills that took oxygen from the water.

❗ FACT-TASTIC

Trilobites lived near the seabed and fed mainly on decaying plant matter and dead animals. They were a favorite prey for a lot of fish.

Cladoselache

KLAD-oh-sel-LAK-ee

Cladoselache was one of the earliest types of sharks. Modern sharks, however, have their mouths underneath the head, whereas Cladoselache had its mouth at the front.

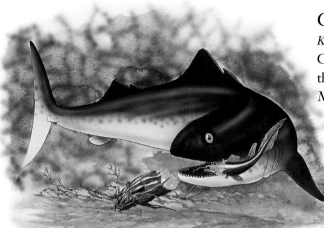

Eusthenopteron

yoos-then-OP-ter-on

Eusthenopteron might have been able to walk on land. Its fins had limblike bone structures and it had lungs for breathing air, as well as gills.

Dunkleosteus

dunk-lee-OH-stee-us

Dunkleosteus did not have any teeth. Instead, it had two razor-sharp bony plates that could shear a fish in half.

Other Prehistoric Animals

Coelacanth
SEE-la-canth

Coelacanths first appeared 400 million years ago, and were rediscovered off the coast of South Africa in 1938.

Megalodon
meg-AL-oh-don

Megalodon was history's most terrifying ocean predator. It was a shark that stretched 56 feet from nose to tail. It would even attack adult whales.

! FACT-TASTIC

Xiphactinus was one of the fiercest creatures in the sea in the Cretaceous period. It had gigantic pointed teeth.

Did you know?
The modern coelacanth's internal organs are unlike those of any modern animal, and its bone structure is just like those seen in ancient fossils.

Xiphactinus
zy-FACT-in-us

Xiphactinus was a giant fish that could grow to 17 feet long and swim at nearly 40 miles per hour.

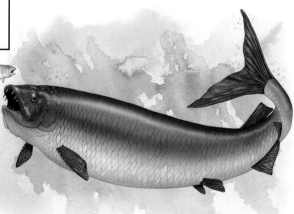

Cacops

KAY-kops

Cacops was an amphibian—it lived both on land and in the water. It had bony plates covering its body for protection.

Diadectes

die-ah-DECK-tees

Diadectes was the first plant-eating animal with a backbone to live on land. It had sharp claws, which it used for digging up plants and roots.

Diplocaulus

DIP-low-cawl-us

Diplocaulus's head shape may have helped it swim more easily, acting like an aircraft's wings as the creature moved through the water.

▶UP CLOSE: **Diplocaulus**

Diplocaulus was a very strange-looking amphibian that lived in the lakes and rivers of North America around 280 million years ago.

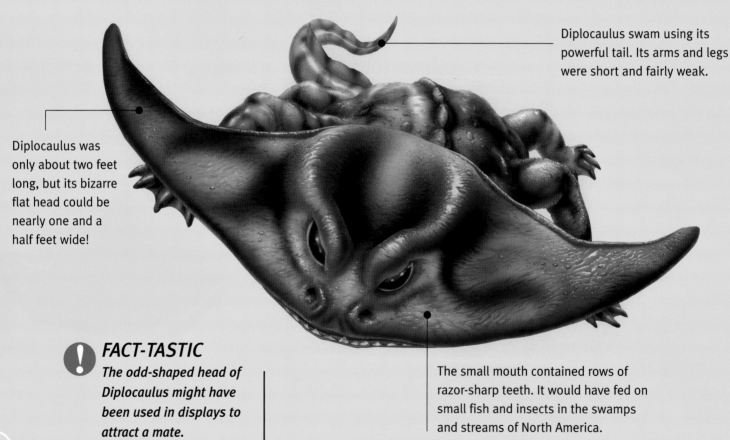

Diplocaulus swam using its powerful tail. Its arms and legs were short and fairly weak.

Diplocaulus was only about two feet long, but its bizarre flat head could be nearly one and a half feet wide!

FACT-TASTIC
The odd-shaped head of Diplocaulus might have been used in displays to attract a mate.

The small mouth contained rows of razor-sharp teeth. It would have fed on small fish and insects in the swamps and streams of North America.

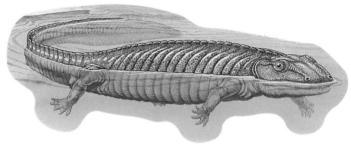

Eogyrinus
EE-oh-ji-RINE-us

Eogyrinus could move from the water to the land. It had short legs, however, so on land its belly would have dragged on the ground.

Ichthyostega
ICK-thee-o-STEG-ah

Ichthyostega looked like a giant newt—it grew up to five feet long. It could move around on land but was more at home in the water.

Eryops
EAR-ee-ops

Eryops hunted like today's crocodiles. It would float just beneath the surface of the water with only its eyes above the surface and then ambush prey at the water's edge.

Other Prehistoric Animals

Coelurosauravus

SEEL-oh-ro-SAWR-ah-vus

Coelurosauravus had two folding wings made of skin. The wings were used to glide between trees while the tail was used as a rudder to provide direction.

Colossochelys

co-LOSS-oh-CHEL-is

Colossochelys was a giant tortoise that measured eight feet long. Its thick, massive shell couldn't be penetrated by even the largest predator's teeth.

Did you know?
Coelurosauravus had wings constructed like paper fans, with skin stretched between hollow, bony struts. No modern animal has wings like this.

Platyhystrix

PLAT-ee-HIS-tricks

Platyhystrix had a large sail on its back. In the morning, the creature would angle the sail toward the sun, picking up the sun's heat and warming its body.

Desmatosuchus

des-mat-oh-SUE-kus

Desmatosuchus had a skull similar to that of a crocodile. Spines covered its entire upper body and the two long shoulder spines grew up to 21 inches long.

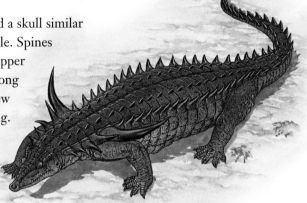

Dimetrodon

die-MET-roh-don

Dimetrodon's large back sail may have been for catching the sun's warmth. Once Dimetrodon had warmed up and its muscles were loose, it would go out to hunt.

Cynognathus

sy-nog-NAY-thus

Cynognathus was a doglike reptile and a fierce predator. Powerful jaws and two long incisor teeth allowed it to tear into its victims.

▶UP CLOSE: **Dimetrodon**

Dimetrodon was a peculiar-looking reptile that lived around 300 million years ago on the dry plains of North America. It was probably the top predator on land at the time.

! FACT-TASTIC

Incredibly, Dimetrodon could be a relative of ours! Mammals originated from primitive reptiles such as Dimetrodon.

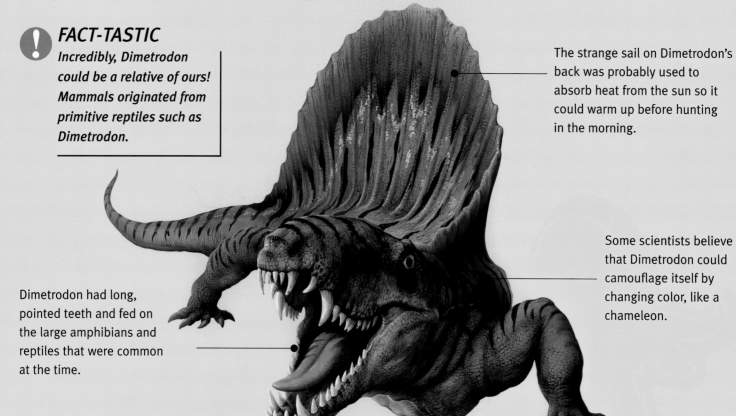

The strange sail on Dimetrodon's back was probably used to absorb heat from the sun so it could warm up before hunting in the morning.

Some scientists believe that Dimetrodon could camouflage itself by changing color, like a chameleon.

Dimetrodon had long, pointed teeth and fed on the large amphibians and reptiles that were common at the time.

Euparkeria

YOO-par-KEE-ree-ah

Euparkeria was less than two feet long
but could run with great speed through
the prehistoric vegetation. It ran on its
hind legs but walked mainly on all fours.

Erythrosuchus

ee-RITH-row-SOOK-us

Erythrosuchus was not a fast-moving
animal, so it hunted large plant-eaters.
At about 15 feet long, it was the largest
land predator of its time.

! FACT-TASTIC

*Although Euparkeria and
Erythrosuchus look a lot
like dinosaurs, they lived
in the Triassic period,
before dinosaurs evolved.*

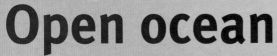

Open ocean

During the Age of Dinosaurs, the oceans were teeming with creatures such as the fearsome Dunkleosteus, and later they were home to huge predators such as Kronosaurus. Create your own prehistoric ocean scene with your stickers.

Other Prehistoric Animals

Gracilisuchus
GRAS-il-i-SOOK-us
Gracilisuchus ate a wide range of animal life, including fish, small lizards, insects, and carrion. Its teeth were shaped like blades and were useful for slicing meat.

Hyperodapedon
HY-per-oh-DAP-ee-don
Fossils of Hyperodapedon have been found as far apart as Scotland and India. Hyperodapedon became extinct when some of its plant foods died out.

Hylonomus
hye-LON-oh-mus
Hylonomus was a lizardlike animal that ate large insects. A Hylonomus fossil was found in what was once a tree stump—the animal had fallen into the hollow stump and became trapped.

Kannemeyria

KAN-ah-MAY-er-ee-ah

Kannemeyria had a large, toothless beak. It used its beak to cut away leaves, shoots, and roots from plants.

Lotosaurus

LOH-to-SAWR-us

Lotosaurus existed around 250 million years ago. It lived off low-lying plants such as ferns and had to eat constantly to nourish its eight-foot-long body.

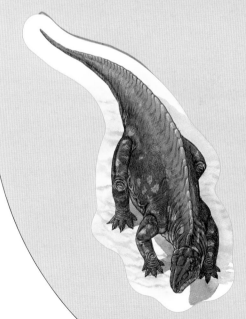

Lagosuchus

LAG-o-SOOK-us

Lagosuchus actually means "rabbit crocodile." It was a very fast runner.

▶UP CLOSE: **Lagosuchus**

Lagosuchus was a tiny animal that lived in South America around 230 million years ago. It was about a foot long and weighed no more than four ounces.

Lagosuchus may have been warm-blooded, which would have helped this small animal survive. Cold-blooded animals cannot feed when the weather is cold.

Lagosuchus fed mainly on tiny reptiles and insects. It used its long, slender arms for catching its prey.

Unlike any reptile today, it moved around on its hind legs only. Its feet were close to its body, like a dinosaur's, rather than sprawled out to the side, like other reptiles' feet.

! **FACT-TASTIC**
Lagosuchus wasn't a dinosaur—but it was a close relative. Scientists can tell this by looking at the ankle bones.

Lycorhinus

LIE-koh-RINE-us

Although Lycorhinus had some long teeth like those found on a dog, it was actually a plant-eater. The incisor teeth were probably used for defense.

Moschops

MOS-kops

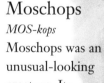

Moschops was an unusual-looking creature. Its shoulders were higher than its hips, so its back sloped steeply downward.

Lystrosaurus

LY-stro-SAWR-us

Lystrosaurus had immensely powerful jaws. Living around swamplands and lakes, Lystrosaurus needed these strong jaws to bite through tough aquatic plants.

Other Prehistoric Animals

Postosuchus
POST-oh-SOO-kus

Postosuchus's back was covered in bony plates that were like armor. It looked similar to a crocodile but was much bigger and could walk on its hind legs.

Scutosaurus
SKOO-toh-SAWR-us

Scutosaurus had a massive body and walked slowly. Its body was so heavy that it needed extra bones in its spine, which was attached to the hips to support the weight.

Did you know?
Some scientists think that Triassic reptiles such as Postosuchus were wiped out by a huge asteroid impact 205 million years ago.

Scaphonyx
ska-FON-iks

Scaphonyx had a large, sharp beak to shear off plant food. The upper and lower jaws locked together, so it had a powerful bite.

Youngina

yung-GUY-nah

Youngina was a small reptile that grew to around 18 inches in length. It fed on snails and insects, and had long fingers and toes for climbing trees.

Shansisuchus

SHAN-see-SOO-kus

Shansisuchus was an ancestor of today's crocodiles. It was a meat-eater and used its powerful jaws to rip off large chunks of meat, which it swallowed whole.

Seymouria

see-MORE-ee-ah

Female Seymouria laid their eggs in water. The young Seymouria hatched in the water, then grew into adults, in the same way that tadpoles grow into frogs.

Other Prehistoric Animals

Elaphrosaurus

el-ah-fro-SAWR-us

Elaphrosaurus had a lightweight body because its bones were hollow. It was a very fast runner, with extremely long and muscular three-toed hind legs.

Deinosuchus

die-no-SUE-kus

Deinosuchus was an enormous creature, yet it swam quickly through the water, powered by thrusts from its immense tail.

Elasmosaurus

eh-LAZZ-mo-SAWR-us

Elasmosaurus's neck stretched to an incredible 26 feet long and contained 72 individual bones. The creature ate fish and squid with its strong jaws and needlelike teeth.

▶UP CLOSE: Deinosuchus

Deinosuchus was a gigantic crocodile that lived in the lakes and rivers of North America around 75 million years ago. It looked very similar to the crocodiles of today but could reach a length of 30 feet and weigh four tons!

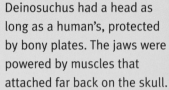

❗ FACT-TASTIC

So far only a few parts of a Deinosuchus skeleton have been found, but scientists have been able to estimate its size.

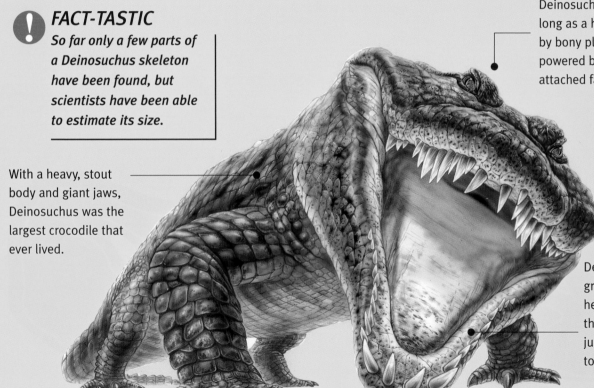

Deinosuchus had a head as long as a human's, protected by bony plates. The jaws were powered by muscles that attached far back on the skull.

With a heavy, stout body and giant jaws, Deinosuchus was the largest crocodile that ever lived.

Deinosuchus would grab its prey by the head and drag it into the water to drown it, just like crocodiles today.

Other Prehistoric Animals

Henodus

HEN-oh-dus

Henodus was a turtlelike creature that ate fish, crustaceans, and mollusks. It had no teeth in its head, but its jaws were strong enough to crack shellfish open.

Kronosaurus

KRON-oh-SAWR-us

A third of Kronosaurus's 30-foot body length was taken up by its head. The teeth were up to 10 inches long, and it would kill prey with a single, crushing bite.

! FACT-TASTIC

Fossilized Kronosaurus remains have been found at only one site, in Queensland, Australia. The first discovery was in 1889.

Libonectes

li-bon-NECK-tees

Libonectes grew up to 50 feet long. Its jaws had overlapping teeth that protruded outside the mouth. These formed a "cage" in which it trapped fish.

Liopleurodon

LIE-oh-PLOOR-oh-don

Liopleurodon was a terrifying fish. Growing up to 50 feet long, it ate crocodiles and sharks as part of its diet.

Mesosaurus

MESS-oh-SAWR-us

Mesosaurus used to live in freshwater lakes and ponds. It was a small, slim creature measuring up to three feet long, and had the webbed digits and flattened tail that are typical of a fast swimmer.

Mosasaur

MOSS-a-SAWR

Mosasaurs had flattened tails. The shape meant the tail acted like a huge paddle, giving the Mosasaur plenty of thrust through the water.

▶UP CLOSE: **Liopleurodon**

Liopleurodon was a marine reptile belonging to the group called plesiosaurs. They had a compact, barrel-shaped body and their arms and legs had evolved into wide flippers for swimming.

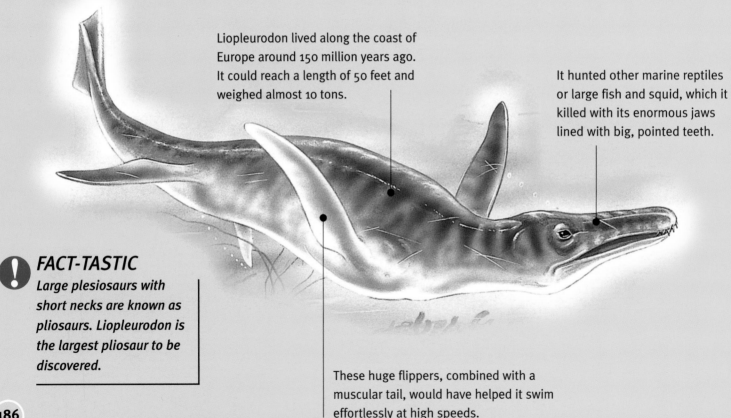

Liopleurodon lived along the coast of Europe around 150 million years ago. It could reach a length of 50 feet and weighed almost 10 tons.

It hunted other marine reptiles or large fish and squid, which it killed with its enormous jaws lined with big, pointed teeth.

! *FACT-TASTIC*
Large plesiosaurs with short necks are known as pliosaurs. Liopleurodon is the largest pliosaur to be discovered.

These huge flippers, combined with a muscular tail, would have helped it swim effortlessly at high speeds.

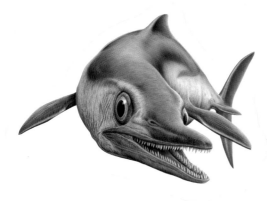

Opthalmosaurus

op-THAL-mo-SAWR-us

Opthalmosaurus gave birth to live young while swimming underwater. The creature had exceptionally big eyes—each one was about four inches wide.

Nanchangosaurus

nan-CHANG-oh-SAWR-us

Nanchangosaurus was an air-breathing reptile that lived in the sea. It had to swim to the surface every once in a while and take a breath of air before diving again.

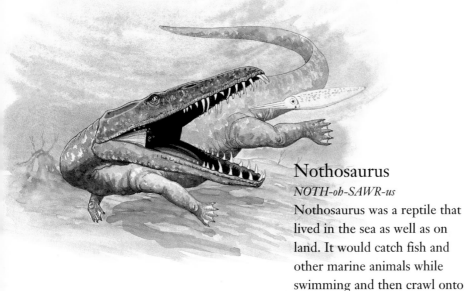

Nothosaurus

NOTH-oh-SAWR-us

Nothosaurus was a reptile that lived in the sea as well as on land. It would catch fish and other marine animals while swimming and then crawl onto land to rest and digest its food.

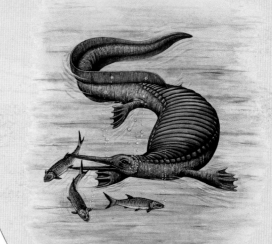

Other Prehistoric Animals

! **FACT-TASTIC**

Shonisaurus was part of a group called ichthyosaurs. Many fossil ichthyosaurs have been found—one was 75 feet long!

Tanystropheus
TAN-ee-STRO-fee-us

Tanystropheus had a very long neck and a useful survival trick. Its tail would snap off if it was grabbed by a predator— and it would grow back later.

Pristichampsus
PRIS-tee-CAMP-sus

Pristichampsus was a 10-foot-long land-dwelling crocodile. Its body was heavily armored with bone, and it ran quickly to catch prey with its vast jaws.

Shonisaurus
SHOW-nee-SAWR-us

Shonisaurus had four flippers and a large, powerful tail. It swam and hunted in packs, and had to come to the surface to take in a breath of air.

Did you know?
Three-quarters of Tanystropheus's body length was taken up by its neck and tail. Its neck was 10 feet long— longer than its body and tail put together.

ankylosaur: a heavy, four-legged dinosaur of the Cretaceous period that was covered in bony armor

antennae: a pair of long feelers that an animal uses to gather information about the surrounding environment

Cambrian: a geologic period in the earth's history, from around 570 to 510 million years ago

ceratopsid: a large, four-legged dinosaur of the Cretaceous period that had a beaked jaw, horns, and a bony frill around the neck

cold-blooded: animals whose body temperature depends on the temperature of the environment

Cretaceous: a geologic period in the earth's history, from around 146 to 65 million years ago

crustacean: a sea creature that has a hard outer shell, no backbone, and a segmented body with appendages

dinosaur: a group of reptiles that lived on earth between 230 and 65 million years ago; the word means "terrible lizard"

duckbill: a dinosaur that had a mouth resembling a duck's beak, which was used for eating leaves and foliage

fossil: the remains of plants and animals that have been preserved in the earth

gastroliths: small stones eaten by an animal in order to help break up food in its stomach

hibernate: to sleep through the winter in a nest or burrow

iguanodont: a dinosaur that generally walked on two legs, ate plants, and had a spiked thumb

incubate: to keep eggs warm until they hatch

Jurassic: a geologic period in the earth's history, from around 210 to 140 million years ago

migrate: to move from one place to another in search of food, a better climate, or breeding grounds

mollusk: a type of animal that has a soft body, no backbone, and a hard outer shell

paleontologist: a scientist who studies prehistoric fossils

parasite: an animal or plant that lives on and feeds off another animal or plant

predator: an animal that hunts and kills other animals for food

prehistoric: the period of earth's history before the introduction of written history

prey: any animal that is hunted for food by a predator

prosauropod: a plant-eating dinosaur that had a long neck, a small head, and walked on all fours

pterosaur: a type of flying reptile that lived from around 228 to 65 million years ago

reptile: a cold-blooded vertebrate animal that lays eggs and has scaly skin

sauropod: an extremely large, four-legged, plant-eating dinosaur with a long neck and a small head

scutes: bony plates on an animal's skin

theropod: a dinosaur that mainly ate meat, moved around on strong hind legs, and lived between 220 to 65 million years ago

Triassic: a geologic period in the earth's history, from around 248 to 206 million years ago

vertebrae: the bones that make up a backbone

vertebrate: a creature that has a backbone

warm-blooded: an animal that keeps its body temperature constant regardless of the temperature of the environment

Index

Index